101
Favorite Dry Flies

HISTORY, TYING TIPS, AND FISHING STRATEGIES

by
David Klausmeyer

Skyhorse Publishing

For Sharon. You make fly tying fun.

Copyright © 2013 by Skyhorse Publishing.

All Rights Reserved. No part of this book may be reproduced in any manner without the express written consent of the publisher, except in the case of brief excerpts in critical reviews or articles. All inquiries should be addressed to Skyhorse Publishing, 307 West 36th Street, 11th Floor, New York, NY 10018.

Skyhorse Publishing books may be purchased in bulk at special discounts for sales promotion, corporate gifts, fund-raising, or educational purposes. Special editions can also be created to specifications. For details, contact the Special Sales Department, Skyhorse Publishing, 307 West 36th Street, 11th Floor, New York, NY 10018 or info@skyhorsepublishing.com.

Skyhorse® and Skyhorse Publishing® are registered trademarks of Skyhorse Publishing, Inc.®, a Delaware corporation.

www.skyhorsepublishing.com

10 9 8 7 6 5 4 3 2 1

Library of Congress Cataloging-in-Publication Data is available on file.

ISBN: 978-1-62087-561-2

Printed in China

Contents

Introduction

Deciphering the Challenge of the Rising Trout

SUCCESSFULLY CASTING A DRY FLY TO A FEEDING TROUT IS the pinnacle of the fly angler's art. The first steps are identifying what the fish is eating, selecting the correct forgery, and choosing the proper position in the river from which to cast. Even the angle of the light and potential shadows that might alarm your quarry must be considered.

You fall into rhythm with the rising trout and the flowing water. You cast the fly just ahead of the fish, and just a moment before it should return to the surface to snatch another winged morsel. You tend the line both before and after it drops to the water. The bits of feather and fur, tied to a piece of bent wire, bob with the speed of the current. You wait and watch.

If you've considered the problem correctly and handled your tackle properly, a slick wet nose will poke through the surface to suck in your fly. You may now consider yourself a good angler. A very accomplished fly fisher can do this repeatedly, intuitively going through the steps that lead to tugs on the end of his line.

It's said that nymphs catch more trout and streamers fool bigger fish, but nothing beats the joy of seeing that wet nose intercept your fly from the top of the water.

This book is about dry flies. Not all dry flies, but *favorite* dry flies—101 flies, to be exact. I have selected some of my favorite patterns, and a group of angling friends chose some of theirs. What follows is a collection of floating flies that will catch trout anywhere.

Each entry contains a clear—and hopefully artful—photograph of the fly, a precise materials recipe, and a small story describing the pattern. Sometimes I tell the history of the fly or offer a few tying or fishing tips. Other times I discuss what the pattern imitates and give a brief lesson in streamside entomology. The material is as varied as the flies themselves.

There's no way a small book can contain *every* favorite fly; in fact, I am including a few patterns that have never appeared in print. But, each fly has been chosen and tied by an experienced angler, the kind of fisherman who can intuitively decipher the challenge of the rising trout.

David Klausmeyer
Spring 2013

Acknowledgments

101 FAVORITE DRY FLIES: HISTORY, TYING TIPS, AND FISHING STRATEGIES contains a fistful of patterns you can use to catch trout wherever they swim. I have included a few of my own flies, but have also relied on the help of many friends in compiling this small collection. They are all expert anglers and fly designers, and when they recommend a pattern, we should all listen.

But I am writing in the present tense, which is not entirely accurate: two of the contributors—Fran Betters and Warren Duncan—are no longer with us. Their influence on fly fishing and tying, however, will remain timeless.

My heartfelt thanks to the following gentlemen (and ladies) for helping with this project:

Tom Baltz
Al and Gretchen Beatty
Fran Betters
Gary Borger
Bill Black
David Brandt
Dennis Charney
Warren Duncan
Jay "Fishy" Fullum
Keith Fulsher
Aaron Jasper

Claes Johansson
Craig Mathews
Dennis Potter
Jesse Riding
Al Ritt
Mike Romanowski
Ted Rogowski
Ed Shenk
Mike Valla
Ken Walrath
Sharon E. Wright

CHAPTER ONE

Matching the Hatch: Mayflies, Caddisflies, and Stoneflies

1

Slow-water, Blue-winged Olive

Hook: Standard dry-fly hook, sizes 20 to 16.
Thread: Olive 8/0.
Tail: Dark pardo Coq de Leon.
Body: Stripped peacock quill, dyed olive.
Thorax: Olive Superfine dubbing.
Wing post: White Hi-Vis polypropylene yarn.
Hackle: Grizzly.

THE SLOW-WATER, BLUE-WINGED OLIVE IS EXTREMELY productive in slow-water scenarios where the trout are ultra selective. The body is very slender, and when combined with a light-wire hook, this pattern is extremely buoyant.

The parachute-style hackle on the Slow-water, Blue-winged Olive makes the fly float on the surface with the body resting in the film like a real emerger. This pattern creates a realistic-looking silhouette on the water, which is necessary when fishing for very discerning trout in slower moving sections of a stream.

Feel free to swap other colors of yarn for the wing post. Hot pink and orange are easy to track on the water—even in failing light, and the fish do not seem to notice these bright colors.

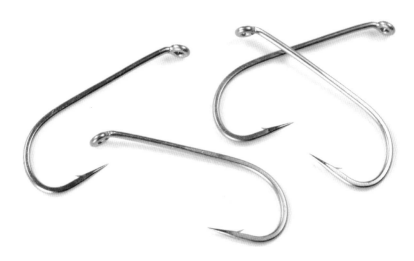

2
Hovering Green Drake Emerger

Hook: Partridge Klinkhamer hook, size 10.
Thread: Brown 6/0.
Tail: Dingy olive marabou tips.
Abdomen: Dingy olive marabou.
Rib: Extra-fine copper wire or clear monofilament.
Thorax: Peacock herl.
Wing bud: Cul de canard.
Hackle: Grizzly, dyed tan, or Cree.
Indicator: Closed-cell foam.

AS AN AUTHOR, IT'S FUN TO SHARE SOME OF YOUR OWN patterns, and this is one of mine—well, sort of. I made several changes to the classic Quigley Cripple, so many, in fact, that most fly designers would claim it as an entirely new pattern. When I look at the Hovering Green Drake Emerger, however, I still see the basic form of Bob Quigley's famous fly, so I think of it as more of a second or third cousin. It's different, but there is no denying the family resemblance.

The tail and feathery abdomen, which hang down in the surface film, do an admirable job of imitating a beefy green drake or *Hexagenia* mayfly nymph. Counter-wrap the rib over the abdomen to protect the marabou fibers. The cul de canard wing bud, full-hackle collar, and foam indicator keep the head of the fly above the water like a real emerger.

Tying the Hovering Green Drake Emerger

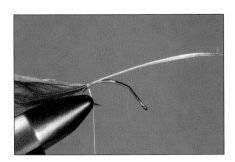

1. Wrap a layer of thread on the end of the hook shank. Strip the fibers from the base of a marabou feather. Tie the bare stem to the hook using two or three loose thread wraps.

2. Pull the marabou to form the tail of the fly. Tighten the thread to lock the marabou to the top of the hook. Tie on a piece of extra-fine copper wire.

3. Twist the marabou into a tight rope. Wrap the twisted feather up the hook to create the abdomen of the fly. Tie off and cut the surplus marabou. Counter-wrap the wire (in the opposite direction of the marabou) to make the rib. Tie off and cut the remaining piece of wire.

4. Tie on a small piece of cul de canard for the wing bud. Strip the excess fibers from the base of a hackle. Tie the feather to the hook.

5. Tie on three or four strands of peacock herl. Wrap the herl on the hook to make the thorax. Tie off and clip the surplus herl. Tie a piece of closed-cell foam to the top of the fly.

6. Wrap the hackle collar. Tie off and cut the remaining hackle tip. Tie off and snip the thread.

3
Carol's Caddis

Hook: Regular dry-fly hook, sizes 20 to 12.

Thread: Size 6/0, color to match the body.

Body: Any dry-fly dubbing, color to match the caddisflies on your local waters.

Underwing: Light gray mallard-flank fibers, slightly longer than the hook shank.

Wing: Natural snowshoe hare foot fur.

JAY "FISHY" FULLUM DESIGNED CAROL'S CADDIS TO HONOR his favorite angling companion, his wife. (Carol Fullum was once a production fly tier, so Fishy's flies have to be spot-on to get her approval.)

In describing the origins of this pattern, Fishy said, "I was replenishing my inventory of caddisflies when Carol took a minute to see what was coming off my vise. She retrieved her vest and checked out her supply of caddisflies. Carol said she had an idea for a simple, durable pattern that she could see on the water. While she hasn't tied flies in many years, she definitely knows what she wants in her patterns."

They have used Carol's Caddis to catch trout in a dozen states. The materials always stay the same, but they change colors and sizes to match the local caddisflies. They recommend sprinkling a little powdered flotant on the fly before fishing.

Dark Visible Dun

Hook: Regular dry-fly hook, sizes 16 to 12.
Thread: Black 8/0.
Tail: Deer body hair.
Body: Stripped peacock quill.
Wing: White calf tail.

FLY-TIER KEITH FULSHER IS ONE OF THE LEGENDS OF FLY fishing of the last half of the twentieth century. His Thunder Creek series of streamers, designed to imitate dace, minnows, and other forms of common baitfish, was his answer to the dry-fly purists' mantra of "match the hatch." While well known for his unique family of streamers, Keith is always eager to fish dry flies when the trout start rising, and I was so pleased to receive a package containing two of his original surface patterns.

Keith wrote about the Dark Visible Dun for the June/July 1962 edition of *The Sportsman*, which was the publication of the Southern New York Fish & Game Association. (Keith included a copy of that article in the package.)

In Keith's cover letter, he said, "Most of my dry-fly fishing was with standard patterns, but sometimes I changed them a bit. For instance, on the Royal Wulff, I always put on a white tail instead of the brown. The Dark Visible Dun has been a good fly and has served me well."

Yarn Wing Dun—Dark Hendrickson

Hook: 2X-long dry-fly hook, size 16 or 14.
Thread: Brown 8/0.
Tail: Dark dun hackle fibers.
Abdomen: Brown dry-fly dubbing.
Thorax: Dark brown dry-fly dubbing.
Hackle: Brown.
Wing and head: Dark gray polypropylene yarn.

BEFORE MAKING THE YARN WING DUN, TIER GARY BORGER bends the first one-third of the hook up about twenty degrees. This makes the fly land on the water thorax first. The bend also anchors the thorax in the surface film and allows the fly to rest on the water like a real insect.

When tying the tail of the Yarn Wing Dun, first wrap a tiny ball of dubbing at the end of the hook shank. Next, tie on the tail. The hackle fibers will splay around the ball of dubbing and improve the fly's appearance and flotation.

Check out the great-looking wing and head; Gary makes these using polypropylene yarn. It's easy to imagine tying the wing, but you must do something to prevent it from collapsing onto the fly when fishing. Gary places a small drop of cement on the base of the wing to stiffen the fibers.

This pattern begs for variations. Swap hook sizes and colors of materials to tie imitations of almost any medium to large mayfly dun.

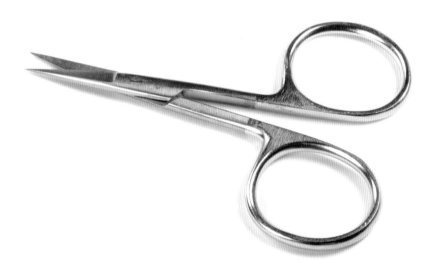

6

Opal & Elk Caddisfly

Hook: Tiemco TMC100, size 12 or 10.
Thread: Fifty-denier, gel-spun thread.
Body: Opal Mirage tinsel.
Rib: Fine gold wire.
Wing: Natural, dark cow elk hair.
Hackle: Dun.

THIS IS DENNIS POTTER'S TAKE ON AL TROTH'S GREAT DRY fly, the Elk-hair Caddis. According to Dennis, the opal tinsel used for the body makes this the best all-round, hackled-caddisfly imitation he has ever used. In fact, he carries no caddis imitations tied with dubbed bodies; they all have opal tinsel bodies. Dennis is so enthusiastic about this pattern that I think it's worth tying and fishing.

Be sure to use a slightly undersized hackle when tying the Elk-hair Caddis, Potter's Opal & Elk Caddis, and similar patterns; the fibers should be equal to or only slightly longer than the width of the hook gap.

Also, Dennis Potter has joined the growing group of tiers using gel-spun thread for making dry flies. They can apply a lot of pressure to the thread and tie durable patterns without adding a lot of bulk.

7

Crowd Surfer Stone

Hook: Regular dry-fly hook, size 8.
Thread: Orange 6/0.
Abdomen: Foam, ribbed with tying thread.
Tails: Brown goose or turkey biots.
Underwing: Tyvek.
Wing: Elk hair and white polypropylene yarn.
Thorax: Bands of orange yarn or dubbing.
Legs: Rubber legs.

THE CROWD SURFER STONE, A PATTERN SOLD BY RAINY'S, is a creation of expert fly-tier Clint Goodman.

The Crowd Surfer Stone is a brilliant, high-floating imitation of the western salmonfly. The foam abdomen makes the pattern almost unsinkable, and the rubber legs give it a great splayed appearance on the surface of the water.

The salmonfly hatch is one of the most anticipated events of the western fishing season. After living in the water for three years, the large nymphs emerge to turn into winged adults; look for the empty cases of the nymphs along the edges of the river. The adults return to the river to mate and lay eggs, and the trout eagerly feed on this smorgasbord of giant insects.

In addition to matching the salmonfly, swap colors and tie the Crowd Surfer Stone to imitate almost any large, adult stonefly.

March Brown Emerger

Hook: Partridge 15BN Klinkhamer, size 14.
Thread: Orange 6/0.
Tail: Three golden, pheasant-tail fibers.
Abdomen: Tannish yellow dry-fly dubbing.
Rib: Stripped center quill from a duck, primary or secondary feather.
Wing: Light dun Hi-Vis yarn.
Thorax: Tannish yellow dry-fly dubbing.
Hackle: Cree or reddish brown and grizzly mixed.

THE STRIPPED MALLARD-QUILL RIB GIVES THIS PARACHUTE March Brown a very realistic appearance. Stripping a mallard quill is easy. Hold a duck pointer or secondary feather with the good side facing up. Nick the center quill near the tip of the feather with a razor blade, creating a small tab. Next, grasp this projecting piece of quill with hackle pliers and pull straight down toward the base of the feather, unzipping the quill. If done properly, you'll get a beautifully segmented quill.

The quill has a tendency to curl as it is stripped, so soak the stripped quill in a bowl of water, and it will straighten nicely. Spend an evening preparing stripped quills for a future tying session. Allow the soaked quills to dry and then store in a plastic sandwich bag.

Blue Dun Snowshoe

Hook: Regular dry-fly hook, sizes 16 to 12.
Thread: Gray 8/0.
Tail: Dun snowshoe rabbit foot fur.
Body: Tying thread.
Wing: Dun snowshoe hare foot fur.
Hackle: Medium dun.

"BLUE DUN" IS A VERY OLD FLY-TYING TERM. THE DISCUSsion of exact shades of color always encourages friendly debate among tiers. With respect to blue dun, think of medium gray with a slightly bluish cast. Flip through the pages of old fly-tying books, and you'll find many other descriptions associated with dun: light dun, medium dun, dark dun, honey dun, and more.

Snowshoe hare fur is a fascinating material. You'll find the cured feet in fly shops in natural cream and a variety of dyed colors. The fur from the bottom of the foot is corkscrewed and holds air bubbles. These bubbles help the Blue Dun Snowshoe and similar patterns float on the surface of the water. This simple pattern is great for novice tiers looking for an easy-to-tie dry fly.

Mahogany Quill Spinner

Hook: Tiemco TMC100, size 12.
Thread: Black 6/0.
Tail: Brown, spade-hackle fibers.
Wings: Light medium dun hen hackles.
Abdomen: Brown neck-hackle, stripped quill.
Thorax: Dark brown dry-fly dubbing.

MAHOGANY MAYFLIES (*ISONYCHIA BICOLOR*) ARE SOME OF the most important insects to fly fishers. *Isonychia* duns molt into spinners within a couple days of hatching, and when they return to mate and lay their eggs, they provide much more concentrated action than during emergence.

Isonychia bicolor mate in swarms twenty to thirty feet in the air. The females usually drop their eggs from high above the water and then fall spent on the surface; this is when they become available to the trout.

Sharon E. Wright's Mahogany Quill Spinner is a fine mayfly imitation. She artfully uses hen-hackle tips to imitate the splayed wings of the natural insect. The stripped-quill abdomen matches the slender profile of a real, adult mayfly.

11
Heckel's Tape Wing Caddis

Hook: 2X-long dry-fly hook, sizes 20 to 14.
Thread: Size 8/0, color to match the body of the fly.
Body: Hare's mask or rabbit dubbing.
Body hackle: Rooster dry-fly hackle.
Wing: Hen-saddle hackle on tape.
Front hackle: Rooster dry-fly hackle.

FLY-TIER BILL HECKEL CREATED THIS UNIQUE PATTERN, and it is sold commercially by the Spirit River Company.

Three things come to mind when regarding this fly.

First, select materials in colors to match the real caddisflies on your local water; black, brown, and tan are the most common. Also, tie this fly in several sizes to match any caddisflies you encounter.

Second, just like when tying an Elk-hair Caddis, the fibers of the body hackle should equal or be slightly shorter than the width of the hook gap.

And third, Heckel places a hen feather on a piece of 3M Scotch Hand Packaging Tape and then clips the wing to shape. Next, he ties the base tip of the trimmed wing to the top of the fly. A roll of tape is inexpensive, and there is enough material to create the wings for dozens of flies. The tape helps the feather hold its shape and creates a durable wing.

Egg-laying Rusty Spinner

Hook: Regular dry-fly hook, sizes 18 to 12.
Thread: Dark brown 6/0.
Tails: Light dun microfibbets.
Egg sac: Yellow embroidery floss.
Abdomen: Turkey biot, dyed rusty brown.
Wing: White McFlylon or polypropylene yarn.
Thorax: Mahogany brown beaver dubbing.

THIS IS OBVIOUSLY A SPINNER IMITATION, BUT WHAT IS A "rusty" mayfly?

This term usually applies to the Baetidae family of mayflies. It is one of the most prolific varieties in North American trout streams. Baetidae often have three generations per year and hatch in impressive numbers.

The genus *Baetis* and its species are often misidentified. Many anglers call them *Baetis*, especially if they're olive in coloration. In reality, the prominent *Baetis* is only one of several very similar and abundant genera in the family Baetidae. Many other anglers call them Blue-winged Olives, but this name is unwittingly applied to dozens of species across several families of mayflies.

Okay, enough of the bug Latin. Suffice it to say that this pattern comes in handy when matching a large number of small mayfly spinners. These spinners, which gather in large numbers over the water, often lead to impressive feeding action from the trout. At times such as these, a spinner imitation will definitely improve your catch rate.

Life & Death Callibaetis

Hook: Daiichi 1100, sizes 18 to 14.
Thread: Tan 8/0.
Tail: Mayfly tails, black barred white.
Abdomen: Gray, stripped quill.
Wings: White organza.
Wing post: Orange Hi-Vis or polypropylene yarn.
Thorax: Adams gray Superfine dubbing.
Hackle: Grizzly.

AL RITT'S LIFE & DEATH CALLIBAETIS IS A FINE IMITATION of a *Callibaetis* spinner. The splayed wings imitate the wings of the real insect and help the pattern float on the surface. Spinner flies are often hard to track on the water, so Al added a wing post of fluorescent orange yarn; you can see this pattern under the poorest lighting conditions.

Callibaetis are part of the Baetidae family of mayflies. Although they are found throughout the United States, the largest concentrations are in the West. Look for *Callibaetis* in the slower sections of rivers and in ponds and lakes.

Although some *Callibaetis* range in hook sizes from 16 to 12, you'll find smaller *Callibaetis* at higher elevations.

ParaNymph

Hook: Regular dry-fly hook, sized to match the natural insects.
Thread: Golden olive 6/0.
Tail: Olive brown Z-Lon or a substitute.
Wing post: Fluorescent orange or lemon yellow calf-body hair.
Body: Natural hare's mask dubbing with plenty of guard hairs.
Hackle: Grizzly.

WHEN MAKING HIS PARANYMPH, TOM BALTZ, WHO IS A right-handed tier, wraps the hackle counter clockwise using articulated hackle pliers and then ties off the feather on top of the hook shank in front of the wing post. He wraps the hackle so the concave side is facing up.

Tom also blends his own hare's mask dubbing. He trims the hair from the ears and center of the mask, but not too much from the cheeks. He blends the fur in a food processor, or he shakes it in a jar of water and then places the material on a piece of newspaper to dry. The body of the fly, Tom says, should be spiky, not smooth.

The ParaNymph is Tom's favorite dry fly. He uses this pattern when fishing by himself and also when guiding in Pennsylvania, and it has caught fish across North America as well as in Patagonia, New Zealand, and South Korea.

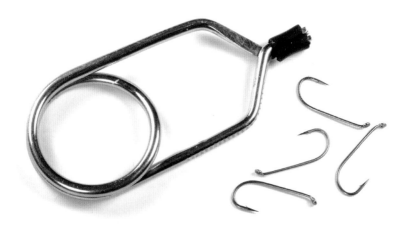

Flight's Fancy

Hook: Regular dry-fly hook, sizes 16 to 12.
Thread: Black 8/0.
Tail: Brown or ginger hackle fibers.
Tip: Gold tinsel.
Wings: Light mallard quill sections.
Body: Pale yellow floss.
Rib: Gold tinsel.
Hackle: Brown or ginger.

NOT ALL FISH-CATCHING DRY FLIES ARE TIED WITH FOAM and rubber legs; the classics still catch their share of trout. Although you won't find Flight's Fancy in the fly boxes of many of today's anglers, it remains an essential pattern that will work on any stream or river.

Flight's Fancy, an English pattern, was named for a Mr. Wright, of Winchester, England, around 1885. The pattern quickly jumped the Atlantic to the United States, and in 1912, Theodore Gordon, the father of American dry-fly fishing, wrote, "Last week I renewed my acquaintance with a native-born dry-fly fisher, who never read a book upon the subject, but picked up his ideas upon the stream. He was troubled because he could get no more flies of a pattern that he had found very killing. You may imagine my surprise when he said that it was called Flight's Fancy."

Closed-cell foam floats forever, and rubber legs give a fly a lot of lifelike wiggling action, but nothing beats the grace and beauty of a pattern such as Flight's Fancy. Even the name is great!

Scuddle Muddle

Hook: Turned-down-eye scud hook, sizes 22 to 10.
Thread: Tan 8/0.
Tag: Tying thread.
Extension fibers: Ginger hackle fibers.
Body: Ginger dry-fly dubbing.
Rib: Tying thread.
Wings: Ginger hackles.
Front hackle: Bleached elk.
Head: Clipped elk hair.

THE SCUDDLE MUDDLE IS ANOTHER OF AL AND GRETCHEN Beatty's original patterns. While they are best known for their outstanding dry flies, the Scuddle Muddle is an emerger. The Beattys also make terrific nymphs and streamers.

I have seen different versions of the Scuddle Muddle, so even the Beattys sometimes swap materials on their flies. For example, rather than elk hair, you can tie what they call the front hackle using deer hair. They also use a variety of colors for body dubbing to make patterns that imitate almost any emerging mayfly or caddisfly. If you wish to tie an extremely small Scuddle Muddle, you can even dispense with the dubbing and dress the body with just thread.

Loop-wing Dun—
Pale Morning Dun

Hook: Regular dry-fly hook, size 16 or 14.
Thread: Gray 8/0.
Tail: Dun hackle fibers.
Abdomen: Gray dry-fly dubbing.
Rib: Brown tying thread.
Thorax: Gray dry-fly dubbing.
Hackle: Dun.
Wing: Gray polypropylene yarn.

THIS IS ANOTHER OF GARY BORGER'S GREAT PATTERNS on which he bends the first one-third of the hook up at a twenty-degree angle before tying the fly.

The looped yarn wing is a neat way to tie small- and medium-size mayfly dun imitations. This style of wing is easy to make. The fibers hold tiny air bubbles, so if the body slips beneath the water, the wing holds the fly close to the surface like an emerger or insect that has failed to emerge. A looped wing also creates a realistic silhouette and is easy to spot on the water. Try experimenting with white, orange, and pink yarn to increase the visibility of your flies. Switch back and forth, and see if the brightly colored wings put off the fish. Let me know how you do.

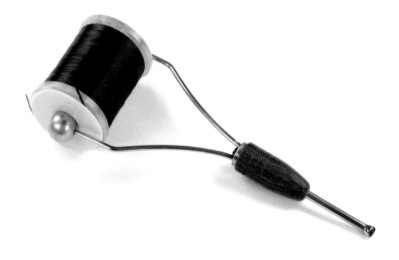

Mahogany Emerger

Hook: Standard dry-fly hook, sizes 20 to 12.
Thread: Dark brown 8/0.
Trailing shuck: Brown Z-lon.
Body: Stripped peacock herl, dyed brown.
Wing: Dun snowshoe hare foot fur.
Thorax: Brown Superfine dubbing

ACCORDING TO CONTRIBUTOR AARON JASPER, HIS Mahogany Emerger "is extremely durable and floats like a cork, even when presented in stream sections with turbulent surface currents."

The snowshoe hare foot fur, which is used for creating the wing of the fly, makes the pattern extremely buoyant. The Mahogany Emerger has a natural appearance when viewed from the bottom. The trailing shuck is very sparse, like the shuck found on the real insect. The stripped peacock herl used for wrapping the abdomen creates a slender, natural-looking body.

Fish the Mahogany Emerger, and any color variations you wish to tie, in both the fast and slow sections of your favorite trout stream. This is a fine choice when the real mayflies are beginning to hatch.

Opal X-Caddis

Hook: Tiemco TMC100, sizes 20 to 14.
Thread: Fifty denier, gel-spun thread.
Trailing shuck: Gold Z-lon.
Body: Opal Mirage tinsel.
Wing: Very fine deer hair.

IT'S SO REFRESHING TO ENCOUNTER A TIER WHO MAKES changes in another fellow's pattern and doesn't claim that he has created a new fly. Dennis Potter freely admits that his Opal X-Caddis is his take on Craig Mathews's great X-Caddis. The addition of the opal tinsel body makes it irresistible to the trout; Dennis says this fly is "ridiculously effective."

Both Craig and Dennis tie these flies in small hook sizes. To do this, you must use sparse amounts of materials. These patterns work well at the beginning of a caddis hatch when the natural insects are just beginning to pop through the surface film. Later in the hatch, when you see real caddisflies skating across the surface, you can switch to an Elk-hair Caddis or a Potter's Opal & Elk.

X-Fly Modular Green Drake

Hook: Regular dry-fly hook, size 10.
Thread: Black 8/0.
Abdomen: Tube Bodiz premade body.
Wings: Medallion Sheeting or a similar wing material.
Hackle: Teal and grizzly.
Head: Black dubbing.

THE X-FLY MODULAR GREEN DRAKE, WHICH IS COMMER-
cially produced by Rainy's, is tied using two unique fly-tying materials.

First, the abdomen, which is a Tube Bodiz, gives the pattern an amaz-
ingly lifelike appearance. Simply tie the Tube Bodiz to the hook and continue making the fly. The abdomen, which is quite sturdy, is hollow and also
adds flotation to the pattern.

The wings are clear Medallion Sheeting clipped into the shape of mayfly
wings. These wings add to the fly's realism and are very durable.

The green drake is a popular summer mayfly, and you will want to stock
up with imitations of this important and large insect. The X-Fly Modular
Green Drake is an ideal candidate for filling that end of your fly box.

21
Isonychia Comparadun

THE BROOK TROUT.

Hook: Tiemco TMC100, size 12 or 10.
Thread: Olive dun 8/0.
Tail: Dun hackle fibers.
Body: Grayish olive dry-fly dubbing, overwrapped with a stripped mallard quill.
Thorax: Grayish olive dry-fly dubbing.
Wing: Dark dun yearling elk

ON HIS HOME WATERS ON THE UPPER DELAWARE RIVER, tier Mike Romanowski says the *Isonychia* mayflies start hatching around the middle of May and continue until the pumpkins are ready for picking. During late spring and early summer, the "Iso's" have a distinct olive cast, and the stripped mallard quill over olive gray dubbing creates the perfect match. The *Isonychia* emergence really comes into its own in July and August, when most other hatches are slim.

Mike sometimes uses fifty denier, fly-tying thread. This allows him to create a very dense yet durable wing, so this pattern floats through the riffles and pocket water where the *Isonychia* live and hatch. Try using the darkest stripped duck quills (black quills are the best) for completing the body on this pattern.

Quill Gordon

Hook: Regular dry-fly hook, sizes 16 to 10.
Thread: Tan 8/0.
Tail: Blue dun hackle fibers.
Body: Stripped herl from the eye of a peacock.
Wing: Wood duck flank fibers.
Hackle: Blue dun.

THE QUILL GORDON HAS BEEN WRITTEN ABOUT MANY times over the decades, but there is no way I can write a book titled *101 Favorite Dry Flies* and not include this famous American pattern; it would be seeded high on any thoughtful angler's list of important floating imitations. How to write about the Quill Gordon in a couple of short paragraphs?

Theodore Gordon, who many consider the father of American dry-fly fishing, created this pattern in the late nineteenth century. Until the creation of the Royal Wulff, it's possible that the Quill Gordon was our most popular dry fly, and its influence has spread beyond fly fishing; there is a bed and breakfast called the Quill Gordon Inn, as well as a fictional detective named Quill Gordon.

Gordon made the body of the fly using a piece of stripped herl from a peacock eye. I might be wrong, but I don't think you'll find stripped peacock herl in any fly shop; you'll have to make your own. Simply pull a piece of herl between your index finger and the nail of your thumb; the nail will strip the flue from the quill. Or, spread the herl between the thumb and index finger of one hand, and remove the flue using a common pencil eraser.

Olive Snowshoe Baetis Spinner

Hook: Regular dry-fly hook, size 18 or 16.
Thread: Olive 8/0.
Tail: Medium dun Microfibbets.
Abdomen: Tying thread.
Wing: Light cream or bleached snowshoe hare foot fur.
Thorax: Natural snowshoe hare foot fur.

BAETIS MAYFLIES ARE WIDESPREAD ACROSS NORTH AMER-
ica. There are several species of Baetis, and in some locations they are one
of the highlights of the fishing season. The small spinners, returning to the
water to lay their eggs, can encourage surprisingly large fish to rise.

Ken Walrath used a synthetic material called Microfibbetts for the
splayed tails on his Olive Snowshoe Baetis. Another product you'll also find
in your local fly shop, called simply Mayfly Tails, is an ideal substitute. Or, if
you wish, you can use the bristles from a fine-fibered paintbrush.

The splayed wings imitate the appearance of a spinner mayfly lying
exhausted on the water.

Green Drake Fan Wing

Hook: Regular dry-fly hook, size 6.
Thread: Olive green 8/0.
Tail: Moose-body hair.
Body: Insect green floss.
Rib: Brown floss.
Wings: Mallard-flank feathers.
Hackle: Grizzly.

WE USE SEVERAL MATERIALS TO TIE THE WINGS ON MAYFLY dun imitations; hair, yarn, and feather fibers are among the most popular ingredients. Sharon E. Wright used mallard-flank feathers to fashion the wings on her Green Drake Fan Wing, and the effect is outstanding.

Feather fan wings look great; they give a fly an appearance of realism. They also help the pattern land upright on the surface of the water; the wings catch the air like a parachute, and the fly plops down in the correct position.

Practice tying fan wings on larger flies such as the Green Drake, and work progressively smaller as you gain experience. You will be limited by the size of the feathers you can find, but you should be able to work down to about size 12.

25 & 26
Crystal Wing Parachute
Pheasant-tail and Adams

Crystal Wing Parachute Pheasant-tail
Hook: Curved-shank emerger hook, sizes 18 to 14.
Thread: Black 6/0.
Tail: Three ring-necked, pheasant-tail fibers.
Abdomen: Ring-necked, pheasant-tail fibers.
Rib: Clear monofilament.
Thorax: Peacock herl.
Wing: Pearl Crystal Splash.
Hackle: Brown.

Crystal Wing Parachute Adams
Hook: Regular dry-fly hook, sizes 18 to 12.
Thread: Gray 6/0.
Tail: Moose-body hair.
Body: Adams gray fine and dry dubbing.
Wing: Pearl Crystal Splash.
Hackle: Brown and natural grizzly.

THESE TWO FLIES DEMONSTRATE THAT YOU CAN ADAPT new materials to update older patterns. Here, the folks at the Spirit River Company have tied the wings on these two common parachute flies using their product, called Crystal Splash. The trout don't mind the change in materials, and these flies are easy to track on the water.

Look at the standard patterns you are already tying. Can you improve any of them using modern materials? Can you make changes in the bodies, wings, or other features? Don't go crazy; just make sensible substitutions and try your new creations the next time you go fishing. This sort of experimenting is fun, and it will keep your tying fresh and exciting.

CRYSTAL WING PARACHUTE PHEASANT-TAIL

CRYSTAL WING PARACHUTE ADAMS

Struggling Green Drake

Extended Abdomen
Base: Flymen Fishing Company Wiggle Shank.
Thread: Olive 8/0.
Tail: Moose hair.
Abdomen: Blue-winged Olive Superfine dubbing.
Rib: Hopper yellow 8/0 tying thread.

Thorax
Hook: Tiemco 2488, sizes 16 to 12.
Extended-body connection: 4X fluorocarbon tippet.
Wing: Black snowshoe hare fur from the back of the foot.
Thorax: Blue-winged Olive Superfine dubbing.
Hackle: Speckled badger or dark champagne.

THE STRUGGLING GREEN DRAKE IS AN UNUSUAL extended-body emerger imitation. Al Ritt ties the abdomen on a Wiggle Shank, a product of the innovative Flymen Fishing Company. Al then places a hook in the vise and attaches the abdomen to the shank; he leaves enough play so the abdomen moves freely. When fishing, the abdomen hangs down in the surface film while the thorax remains on the surface. The Struggling Green Drake does a fine job imitating an insect just breaking through the surface film and turning into a winged adult.

Use this design as a guide to creating imitations of other large, emerging mayflies—a Struggling Hexagenia comes to mind.

Harey Dun—
Blue-winged Olive and
Pale Morning Dun

Harey Dun—Blue-winged Olive
Hook: Daiichi 1100, sizes 22 to 16.
Tail: Olive Mayfly Tails.
Abdomen: Olive stripped quill.
Wing: Black snowshoe hare fur from the back of the foot.
Thorax: Blue-winged Olive Superfine dubbing.
Hackle: Grizzly, dyed olive.

Harey Dun—Pale Morning Dun
Hook: Daiichi 1100, sizes 18 to 14.
Tail: Medium dun Mayfly Tails.
Abdomen: Stripped quill, dyed pale morning dun.
Wing: Medium dun snowshoe hare fur from the back of the foot.
Thorax: Pale Morning Dun Superfine dubbing.
Hackle: Dun.

IT'S SURPRISING HOW MANY TIERS ARE TURNING TO snowshoe hare foot fur to tie the wings on their dry flies. It wasn't too many years ago that pattern designers were turning to new synthetic materials to fashion wings; maybe the large number of flies tied with snowshoe fur indicates that they are returning to natural ingredients.

Al Ritt is a master at the fly-tying vise; his patterns have a consistency you find only in the flies of an accomplished tier. Although the Harey Dun is not a parachute pattern, the fur wing will catch the air as the fly falls to the water, and it will land upright every time. The sparse tail and hackle, wrapped over the dubbed thorax, create the delicate impression of a real Blue-winged Olive on the surface film.

HAREY DUN—BLUE-WINGED OLIVE

HAREY DUN—PALE MORNING DUN

CDC X-Caddis

Hook: Regular dry-fly hook, size to match the natural insects.
Thread: Olive or brown 6/0.
Tail: Ginger Z-Lon.
Body: Natural hare's mask dubbing.
Underwing: Natural dun or brown cul de canard.
Wing: Natural deer hair.
Indicator: Fluorescent orange or pink cul de canard.

THIS IS A KNOCK OFF OF THE VENERABLE X-CADDIS, AND IS one of at least three X-Caddis variations in tier Tom Baltz's fly box. This fly ranks number two on his list of top-three dry flies, so you can feel confident it's a dandy.

The cul de canard underwing gives the fly a bit of bounce and life on the water, and the brightly colored indicator allows anglers "of a certain age" to follow it more easily in broken water. Tom uses only powder-type flotants on patterns containing CDC.

Don't hesitate trimming off the tail when trout are taking spent caddisflies; one summer, this altered fly worked quite well on the picky sippers feeding just off the boat ramp at Wolf Creek Bridge on the Missouri River.

Tying the CDC X-Caddis is not difficult. Either pluck CDC fibers off the feather stem by hand or roll the feather up with a CDC tool, fold, and tie on. Tie the deer hair over the underwing, and tie the CDC indicator on top of the deer hair with the tips to the rear, then fold back, and tie down. Wind a bit of dubbing over the bare thread at the head. Whip finish the thread behind the hook eye before trimming the butt ends off the CDC and deer hair.

31
Quick 'n EZY Parachute

Hook: Regular dry-fly hook, sizes 22 to 10.
Thread: Tan 8/0.
Tail: Ginger hackle fibers.
Body: Ginger dubbing.
Rib: Tying thread and dubbing.
Wings: Ginger hackles.
Hackle: Ginger.

AL AND GRETCHEN BEATTY TIE A WHOLE SERIES OF PARA-chute dry-fly imitations using their Wonder Wing technique. In this case, the reverse-hackle wings serve as the wing post, and they wrap the hackle around the base of the wings. The affect is outstanding.

Start tying the larger sizes—12 and 10—to imitate bigger drakes and similar mayflies; substitute colors to match the insects on your local waters. Work progressively smaller as you gain experience. It's hard to believe, but the Beattys tie the Quick 'n EZY Parachute as small as size 22. I hope to be as proficient at the fly-tying vise one day!

Parachute Floating Nymph—Dark Hendrickson

Hook: Regular dry-fly hook, size 16 or 14.
Thread: Brown 8/0.
Tail: Dark dun hackle fibers.
Abdomen: Brown dry-fly dubbing.
Thorax: Dark brown dry-fly dubbing.
Hackle: Brown.
Back: Brown ball of dubbing.

WHEN I ASKED ANGLING-AUTHORITY GARY BORGER TO submit a few of his favorite flies for this book, he asked, "Would you be interested in a floating nymph? I know it's not technically a dry fly, but you fish it at the surface. It's a really important pattern that catches a lot of fish."

When an expert such as Gary says he has a great pattern, we all need to listen.

Fish the Parachute Floating Nymph just as the trout are beginning to rise. You might not spot adult insects on the water, and the fish might not be breaking through the surface; look for swirls just under the surface—the obvious indication that the trout are feeding on the rising nymphs. Within minutes, the nymphs will be in the surface film, shedding their skins and turning into winged adults. The fish will follow them to the surface, and your Parachute Floating Nymph will be lying in wait.

Instead of the ball of dubbing, you can substitute a polypropylene yarn-looped wing. This is the type of wing Gary ties on his Loop-wing Dun. Follow the same tying instructions, but make the wing considerably smaller.

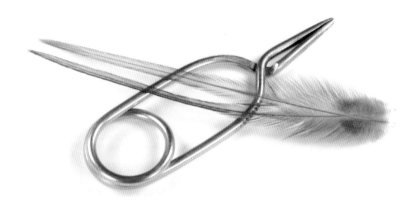

Egg-laying CDC and Elk Caddisfly

Hook: Standard dry-fly hook, sizes 20 to 12.

Thread: Tan 8/0.

Egg sac: Insect green superfine dubbing.

Body: Tan rabbit dubbing.

Collar: Dun cul de canard.

Wing: Coastal deer hair.

WITH RESPECT TO DRY-FLY IMITATIONS OF MOST AQUATIC insects, we should concern ourselves with three stages of development: the emerging nymphs or larvae, crawling through the surface film to turn into adults; the newly hatched, winged adults; and the mating males and egg-laying females. Many anglers are familiar with the spinner stage of mayfly development; this is when the insects return to the water to mate and lay their eggs and then fall exhausted to the surface. Did you ever stop to think that adult caddisflies also go through this stage?

Aaron Jasper used insect green dubbing to fashion the small egg sac on the end of the Egg-laying CDC & Elk Caddisfly. "Perhaps," he says, "it looks like an egg sac, or perhaps the fish just see it as a hot spot like on many of the newest nymphs."

Cul de canard, which is used as a collar, is the real magic of this pattern. The combination of the CDC and deer-hair wing makes the fly extremely buoyant.

Quill-bodied Hendrickson

Hook: Regular dry-fly hook, size 14.
Thread: Brown 8/0.
Tail: Grizzly, dyed tan, or Cree-hackle fibers.
Body: Grizzly, dyed tan, or Cree stripped-hackle quill.
Wing: Wood duck or mallard-dyed wood duck.
Hackle: Grizzly, dyed tan, or Cree.

FOR MANY TROUT ANGLERS ACROSS THE COUNTRY, THE hatch of the Hendrickson mayflies heralds the beginning of the real fishing season. The dainty mayflies ride the surface of the water, and the trout quickly spear this ready meal. The hatches usually occur in mid–May, but the timing shifts forward or back on the calendar by a week or two depending upon location and weather conditions.

With respect to weather, if you hear the Hendricksons are beginning to hatch on your local river, pray for an overcast sky and drizzle for the day you plan to fish. The wet weather prevents the insects from drying their wings and taking flight, and you will see more rising trout and enjoy better dry-fly fishing. If the sky is clear and there is a gentle breeze, the mayflies will quickly dry their wings and take to the air; as a result, you will probably see fewer rising trout, and the fishing might be a little slower.

The Quill-bodied Hendrickson is a Catskill inspired pattern that I have been tying for many years. I have outstanding success using it to catch Maine, landlocked salmon on my home waters. (I'm praying for a cool, overcast, and drizzly spring!)

X-Fly Parachute Adams

Hook: Regular dry-fly hook, size 16.
Thread: Black 8/0.
Abdomen: Tube Bodiz premade body.
Thorax: Gray dry-fly dubbing.
Wing post: White closed-cell foam.
Hackle: Brown and grizzly.

THIS SIZE 16 X-FLY PARACHUTE ADAMS IS ONE OF THOSE flies that makes me shake my head and say, "How'd they do that?" It is small yet perfectly tied, and it is ideal for matching most of the little, dun-colored mayflies you'll find on your local waters.

The abdomen of the X-Fly Parachute Adams is a small, gray Tube Bodiz. These premade bodies, which you can purchase at many fly shops, help in constructing bantam-weight patterns. The white, foam wing post creates a speck on the water so you can easily follow the fly.

Fish the X-Fly Parachute Adams using a long, fine leader and a three- or four-weight rod. Cast this pattern to rising trout, and you'll enjoy fine success.

36
Delaware Hendrickson Emerger

Hook: Tiemco TMC2488, size 14.
Thread: Dark brown 8/0.
Tail: Dark brown Antron.
Abdomen: Mahogany brown turkey biot.
Wing: Dark dun Hi-Vis yarn.
Thorax: Red quill Superfine dubbing.
Hackle: Grizzly, dyed tannish olive.

ACCORDING TO TIER MIKE ROMANOWSKI, "THIS IS PERHAPS the most effective Hendrickson imitation I have ever used."

The Klinkhamer design creates the illusion of an emerging dun, struggling to free itself from its nymphal shuck. One lucky angler, fishing this fly in the annual Delaware River One Bug Tournament, landed more than 120 inches (that's ten feet!) of trout in one day on this fly.

When tying the Delaware Hendrickson Emerger, try using the darkest turkey biots possible; they should be almost black at the base. Although Mike specifies tannish grizzly hackle, feel free to substitute with medium dun; this does not reduce the fly's effectiveness.

Mike did an outstanding job tying this pattern.

Batten Kill Badger

Hook: Regular dry-fly hook, size 12.
Tail: Badger-guard hairs.
Body: Dark muskrat fur dubbing.
Wing: Badger-guard hairs.
Hackle: Silver badger.

CATSKILL FLY-TYING AUTHORITY MIKE VALLA CREATED THE Batten Kill Badger in the late 1970s for fishing during the late evening on the New York State section of the Batten Kill, upstream from Greenwich, New York. Mike says that this pattern is easy to track on the water in the dim light. Even though it has a fairly realistic form, he says he did not tie it to match any particular natural insect; he calls it a "searcher" or "tempting" dry fly.

The white-tipped tail and wings, fashioned using badger-guard hair, look outstanding.

Adams Snowshoe

Hook: Regular dry-fly hook, size 16 or 14.
Thread: Black 8/0.
Tail: Black snowshoe hare foot fur.
Body: Gray snowshoe hare foot fur.
Wing: White or bleached snowshoe hare foot fur.
Hackle: Coachman brown and grizzly.

THIS FLY, TIED BY KEN WALRATH, IS ANOTHER PLEASANT surprise. This time he blended snowshoe hare foot fur and a classic design—the Adams—to create a very cool fly.

The Adams Snowshoe, featuring a tail, body, and wing all tied using the fur, floats high and dry over the roughest water. This pattern will bob along while other standard flies get sucked under the surface.

It seems like Ken is challenging us to think and experiment. Nothing requires us to remain hidebound to established pattern recipes. What other patterns can we improve using snowshoe hare foot fur?

UV2 Parachutes

Hook: Regular dry-fly hook, sizes 20 to 12.
Thread: White 8/0.
Tail: Hackle fibers.
Underbody: Pearl Flashabou.
Abdomen: Turkey biot.
Thorax: Fine & Dry UV2 dubbing.
Wing: Turkey flat feather.
Hackle: Rooster.

TIE UV2 PARACHUTES IN COLORS AND SIZES TO MATCH THE adult mayflies on your local waters; this design lends itself to imitating almost all small- to medium-size duns.

UV2 is a new line of products from the Spirit River Company. According to Spirit River, UVF is the fluorescent wavelength in bright colors we see, and it allows fish to see flies and lures from great distances. UVR, which stands for ultraviolet reflectance, is the UV light humans cannot see; insects and animals, however, can see UVR. In fact, according to Spirit River, the females of most species recognize the UVR signature of males. Spirit River has developed a way to process materials with both UVF and UVR wavelengths, which they call UV2.

Spirit River recommends wrapping a base layer of pearl or silver Mylar tinsel or white thread before wrapping UV2 dubbing or other material onto the hook. Doing this, they say, allows the UV light spectrums to reflect out of the pattern.

Is UV2 for real or just another form of hype? It's hard to tell. There is no denying the fact, however, that many anglers believe adding chartreuse to a streamer improves the fly's ability to catch fish. I believe this myself, and Bob Clouser, the creator of the Clouser Minnow, is fond of saying, "It ain't no use if it doesn't have chartreuse."

To this day, I have never seen anything in nature that is chartreuse.

Yarn Wing Caddis

Hook: Regular dry-fly hooks, sizes 18 to 12.
Thread: Black 8/0.
Body: Black dry-fly dubbing.
Hackle: Black.
Wing: Black polypropylene yarn.

GARY BORGER'S YARN WING CADDIS IS A SNAP TO TIE; I can't imagine anything easier. It also requires only a couple of ingredients: hook and threads (just like any fly), dubbing, polypropylene yarn, and a hackle. You'll find all of these materials in your neighborhood fly shop. Gary Borger sent a black version of this fly, but you can substitute colors to tie imitations of any caddisfly you find on the water.

Note that this is not a great pattern for skating across the surface; the Elk-hair Caddis and some other flies are better choices for more active presentations. The Yarn Wing Caddis rests lower in the water. What it lacks in this one category, it makes up for in its simplicity. Any new tier can make the fish-catching Yarn Wing Caddis.

Not Spent Spinner

Hook: Standard dry-fly hook, sizes 20 to 10.
Thread: Dark brown 8/0.
Egg sac: Sulphur orange Superfine dubbing.
Tails: Coq de Leon.
Body: Stripped peacock herl, dyed brown.
Wing: Cul de canard.
Thorax: Brown Superfine dubbing.

THE NEXT TIME YOU'RE ON THE WATER AND THE AIR IS FULL of spinner mayflies, catch a few of the swarming insects in your hat. Carefully examine the dainty insects, and you will probably see that a couple of them—the females—have brightly colored egg sacs on the tips of their abdomens. The Not Spent Spinner imitates this stage of mayfly development.

The sulphur-orange dubbing mimics the egg sac of a real mayfly, and the stripped peacock herl creates a slender abdomen. Cul de canard, used for the wings, makes the fly almost unsinkable; this is important because the majority of spinner falls last from early evening into the dark of night, and you might not be able to see whether your fly is floating or has become waterlogged and sunk.

Hi-Tie Sally

Hook: Regular dry-fly hook, size 12.
Thread: Yellow 8/0.
Wing: Elk hair.
Egg sac: Thread floss.
Body: Bright yellow or lime floss.
Hackle: Ginger.

YELLOW AND LIME SALLIES ARE COMMON STONEFLIES throughout much of the United States. Generally appearing in June, the mating flights of these small insects can generate mighty rises from some of the largest trout in the river.

Make the wing on this pattern using the "hi-tie" method. In this case, fashion the wing in three parts. First, wrap a small section of the body at the end of the hook shank and tie on a very small bunch of elk hair. Next, wrap the second body section and add a second bunch of hair. Finally, add the third sections of the body and wing. Take care not to crowd the hook eye; leave ample room to wrap a full, high-floating hackle collar.

Cream Comparadun

Hook: Tiemco TMC100, sizes 14 to 10.

Thread: Primrose 8/0 or gel-spun thread.

Tail: Cream hackle fibers.

Body: A double layer of yellow Krystal Flash covered with cream dry-fly dubbing.

Wing: Bleached yearling-elk hair.

THIS FLY NEEDS NO INTRODUCTION. THE COMPARADUN series of flies, popularized by Al Caucci and Bob Nastasi, has become world famous for its effectiveness for fooling selective trout.

Tier Mike Romanowski, who made this Comparadun, offered these tying tips.

"One area where the use of gel-spun thread has facilitated the tying process is in its application when tying hair flies. The use of fifty denier GSP thread has allowed me to almost double the amount of hair I use for the wings while eliminating the bulk associated with using such large quantities of material. Make sure the thread is heavily waxed, because it is pretty slippery stuff. When tying down the wing, make a few loose wraps and then gradually increase tension on subsequent wraps until you reach maximum pressure—*your* maximum, that is, because you never have to worry about breaking the thread. This results in a highly buoyant and durable wing that will keep its shape for the life of the fly.

"I've also taken a page out of the Dick Talleur's handbook and wrap a double layer of yellow Krystal Flash on the shank before applying the dubbing. The flash makes the body 'glow' when wet, and prevents the hook from darkening the dubbing."

Hock-wing Sulphur

Hook: Turned-up-eye dry-fly hook, your choice of sizes.
Thread: 8/0.
Tail: Light tan or cream guard hairs from a red fox.
Body: Blend of pale-yellow-dyed seal's fur dubbing (or a substitute) mixed with cream red fox fur dubbing.
Wing: Hock feather tips from a hen or rooster, natural or dyed dun.
Hackle: Light or medium ginger.

MIKE VALLA DESIGNED THE HOCK-WING SULPHUR FOR fishing the Owasco Inlet in central New York State. The Owasco is a tributary of Owasco Lake, one of the smaller Finger Lakes. Rainbow trout run the stream in the spring, and some fish hang around into May before migrating back downstream to the lake.

The Hock-wing Sulphur gets its name from the two small feathers, found on the hock (ankle) area of a chicken, used to make the wings of the fly. Mike has never liked cut wings on sulphur imitations, and he says that dry-fly hackle tips seem too narrow to simulate wings found on the natural insects.

The body is seal's fur dubbing mixed with cream red fox fur. This inspiration came from Jack Atherton's classic book, *The Fly and the Fish*, which was published in 1951. Atherton favored the natural sheen of seal's fur, but as he admitted, it's not an easy material to spin alone, so he blended it with fox fur. Today, you will probably have to select a substitute for real seal's fur.

Black's Lipstick Spinner

Hook: Light-wire, curved-shank emerger hook, sizes 18 to 12.
Thread: Size 6/0.
Abdomen: V Tube. (You can substitute with another brand of narrow-diameter tubing.)
Tails: Microfibbets or Mayfly Tails.
Thorax: Fine & Dry dubbing.
Wing post: Closed-cell foam post with a bright top.
Wings: 0.5-millimeter-thick, closed-cell foam, clipped to shape.
Hackle: Rooster.

BILL BLACK, THE HEAD HONCHO OF SPIRIT RIVER, INC., doesn't just sell fly-tying materials; he is also a good fly designer.

This pattern is Bill's Lipstick Spinner. To be honest, I didn't understand the name of the pattern until I took this photograph; the foam wing posts do look like tubes of lipstick.

The abdomens are small-diameter tubing with Microfibbets glued into the ends to create tails. The hackles, wing posts, and foam wings keep the flies floating on the surface of the water. The bright yellow tabs at the end of the posts make it easy to see these flies on the water.

This is another pattern you can tie in different sizes and colors to match the real spinner mayflies on your local waters.

Yellow Adams (Sort Of)

Hook: Regular dry-fly hook, size 14.
Thread: Tan or orange 6/0.
Wings: Grizzly hen-hackle tips
Tails: Coq de Leon or grizzly throat-hackle fibers.
Body: Light yellow rabbit fur with a bit of orange blended in.
Hackle: Dun Cree, barred rusty dun, golden grizzly, or light-barred ginger.

THIS IS A REALLY NICE PATTERN THAT SUGGESTS A CRANE fly, as well as various mayfly duns and spinners. It is a delicate change of pace for general dry-fly fishing. Use it during low water as an alternative to terrestrial patterns. This version is a little lighter in overall appearance than a traditional Adams and is a good fly for late spring, summer, and early fall fishing on either limestone or freestone streams.

If you don't have the hackles listed in the pattern recipe, use a light ginger and a grizzly hackle; wrap one feather at a time.

EZY Occasion—
Double Magic

Hook: Down-eye scud hook, sizes 22 to 10.
Thread: Tan 8/0.
Tag: Tying thread with light blue dubbing.
Body: Ginger dubbing.
Rib: Tying thread with light blue dubbing.
Wings: Ginger hackles.
Hackle: Brown.

THE EZY OCCASION—DOUBLE MAGIC IS AN ADAPTATION
of a Gary LaFontaine pattern called simply the Occasion. The major dif-
ference is that Al and Gretchen Beatty have added their Wonder Wings to
the fly.

"The original Occasion was one of three similar emerger imitations
that I remember," Al said. "It was a real killer pattern. We used to get
together to fish with Gary, and we would use his flies and just catch a lot
of trout."

The EZY Occasion—Double Magic is designed to ride with the body
hanging down in the water, as seen in the photograph. The hackle holds the
head and wings above the surface. This pattern mimics an emerger breaking
through the surface and turning into a winged adult.

Olive CDC Caddisfly

Hook: Standard dry-fly hook, sizes 20 to 14.
Thread: Olive 8/0.
Body: Olive superfine dubbing.
Wing: Dun cul de canard.
Head: Dun cul de canard.

THE OLIVE CDC CADDISFLY IS VERY SIMPLE TO TIE YET IS AN extremely productive fly. The cul de canard, used to make the wing and head of the fly, makes it nearly unsinkable.

The origins of this style of pattern are more European than American. Rather than adding a lot of bells and whistles to their flies, many European tiers take a bare-bones approach, emphasizing the overall form of their patterns. The Olive CDC Caddisfly strikes the right posture on the water, and the cul de canard keeps it riding high and dry.

For making the head of the fly, Aaron Jasper inserted a cul de canard feather between the strands of the flat-waxed tying thread using a device called The Magic Tool. (Look for The Magic Tool in your local fly shop.) He then wrapped the thread and CDC on the hook as a collar. Switzerland's Marc Petijean created this nifty tying technique and The Magic Tool.

Transducer—Pale Morning Dun

Hook: Curved-shank nymph or caddis-larva hook, size 16.
Thread: Yellow 8/0.
Tail: Mottled hackle fibers.
Abdomen: Pheasant-tail fibers.
Rib: Narrow pearl Flashabou.
Head of nymph: Peacock herl.
Nymph legs: Mottled hackle-fiber tips.
Emerger body: Yellow dry-fly dubbing or tying thread.
Wing post: Fine hair of your choice.
Hackle: Light dun.

UTAH'S SAM SWINK CREATED THIS COOL PATTERN. THE Transducer is unusual in that it is really two flies in one. Check out the photos, and you'll see what I mean.

The first half of the fly is an imitation of a nymph; this part of the pattern hangs down in the surface film. The front portion of the Transducer is a bare-bones mayfly dun imitation: a simple body, wing post, and parachute hackle.

The Transducer is designed to mimic a mayfly emerging out of its nymph skin and turning into a winged adult.

This version of the Transducer is tied in the colors of a Pale Morning Dun, but you can substitute materials to tie imitations of all your favorite mayflies.

Sulphur Cripple

Hook: Tiemco TMC100, sizes 22 to 14.
Thread: Primrose 8/0.
Tail: Cream hackle fibers.
Abdomen: Sulphur turkey biot.
Wing: Two white hen-hackle tips.
Thorax: Sulphur orange Superfine dubbing.
Hackle: Pale yellow or cream.

THIS IS A VARIATION OF A FLY SHOWN TO TIER MIKE Romanowski by Bighorn-guide Bob Krumm more than twenty years ago. Since then it has become one of the few sulfur imitations he carries. The key to this fly's effectiveness is its ability to represent a cripple, dun, or spinner. Mike sets the wings slightly back on the shank so he can X-wrap the dubbing underneath the shank *after* wrapping the hackle. This pulls the hackle fibers up to the sides of the fly, resulting in a dense area of hackle on the sides of the body, providing superior flotation.

Don't worry too much about the position of the wings; you want this fly to look like a dying dun or spinner. It's tough to find biots that are light colored enough to imitate the abdomen of a sulfur, so Mike buys white biots and dyes them for about thirty seconds in yellow Rit dye.

Cahill Quill

Hook: Regular dry-fly hook, sizes 16 to 10.
Thread: Tan 8/0.
Tail: Ginger hackle fibers.
Body: Stripped herl from the eye of a peacock.
Wing: Wood duck flank fibers.
Hackle: Ginger.

THE LIGHT CAHILL (THERE IS A SEPARATE FLY PATTERN BY that name) is one of our most dependable summer mayflies. In some areas, the duns have a tendency to emerge throughout the day, and the trout never seem to key in to them; in other locations, you might encounter a more vigorous hatch that gets the fishes' attention.

There are many patterns designed to imitate the light Cahill insects, and the Cahill Quill is certainly a member of that family. Mike Valla's rendition of this important pattern is delicate and perfectly proportioned; use it as a model when tying your own Cahill Quills.

A note about tying with stripped-peacock herl: although the body of the finished fly has a lovely segmentation, the herl is not very durable. Place a drop of cement on the thread underbody before wrapping the herl, or place a drop of cement on the completed herl body. Either method increases the durability of the body.

Making Split Flank-feather Wings

There are a couple of ways to tie lovely Catskill-style wings. Wood duck feathers are more expensive that dyed mallard, so some tiers place one wood duck feather on the hook and then divide the fibers in half to create the two wings. Traditionally, tiers used two feathers placed back-to-back.

Since this information is going into a book, and it will live forever, I will use two real wood duck feathers. (Besides, I hunt ducks, and I'll collect more wood duck flank feathers this autumn.)

1. Place the two feathers together with the tips even. Strip the excess fibers from the bases of the feathers. Tie the bare stem to the top of the hook using two or three loose thread wraps. Draw the feathers toward the rear of the fly until the wing fibers are the proper length; keep the feathers on top of the shank while you work. Lock the feathers in place with several tight thread wraps.

2. Some tiers cut the butt ends even, but this will create a hump and perhaps an uneven finished body. I prefer cutting the butt ends of the feathers at different lengths. Later, when we wrap the thread to the end of the hook, this will create a more level underbody.

3. Pinch the wing fibers upright. Wrap a small dam of thread in front of the fibers to hold them up. Mike Valla, whose terrific flies you'll find in the book, prefers making a tall wing, and I follow his method; the height of the wing about matches the length of the hook shank.

4. Divide the fibers in half to create the two wings. Make several figure-eight wraps between the wings.

5. Wrap the thread to the end of the hook shank. We have a level underbody for making the rest of the pattern.

October Irresistible Caddis

Hook: Regular dry-fly hook, size 12.
Thread: Orange gel-spun.
Body: Orange deer hair.
Hackle: Brown.
Wing: Elk hair.
Antennae: Fine, brown monofilament.

THE CADDISFLIES OF THE GENUS *DICOSMOECUS*, WHICH are referred to as the fall or October caddis, are considered one of the West's caddis super hatches. The hatches of these large insects, which average about thirty millimeters long, are concentrated within a two- to three-week period. The October caddis emerges in low, clear water and is most active during the afternoon and early evening.

The classic Irresistible has an upright wing, a full-hackle collar, and a tan, spun-and-clipped, deer-hair body; only accomplished tiers care to make this sort of complicated body. The October Irresistible Caddis is a variant of this older pattern, and it, too, will appeal to experienced fly tiers.

I recommend using fifty- or one hundred-denier, gel-spun thread for making this pattern. Gel-spun thread is super strong and is perfect for spinning deer hair and keeping bulk to a minimum. If you cannot find orange gel-spun thread, use white gel-spun thread and swipe an orange permanent marker on the last two inches of thread when tying the head.

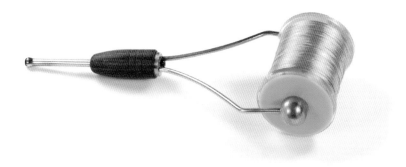

Bradley Special

Hook: Regular dry-fly hook, sizes 16 to 12.
Thread: Red 8/0.
Tail: Brown hackle fibers.
Body: Red squirrel dubbing, spun in a dubbing loop of red tying thread.
Wing: Wood duck flank fibers.
Hackle: Brown.

ACCORDING TO LEGEND, THE BRADLEY SPECIAL WAS devised by Catskill-anglers William Chandler and William Bradley. Roy Steenrod and Harry Darbee, two of the Catskill's most legendary tiers, also claimed that William Chandler developed the famed Light Cahill. The Dette family, longtime local tiers, added the Bradley Special to their lineup of patterns they dressed for visiting anglers.

The Bradley Special is important, because it demonstrates using the color of the thread to influence the appearance of the completed body; if you look closely, you can see the red thread peeking through the body dubbing. This effect becomes even more pronounced when the fly is wet. Important note: consider using white thread if you do not want the color to show up on the finished fly; white thread turns translucent when wet. Any other color of thread, especially darker hues, will have a profound effect on the completed pattern.

54
A.J.'s Hi-Vis Sulphur Emerger

Hook: Standard dry-fly hook, sizes 20 to 14.
Thread: Yellow 8/0.
Tail: Brown Z-Lon.
Body: Sulphur orange Superfine dubbing.
Thorax: White hackle.
Wing post: White Hi-Vis polypropylene yarn.

A.J.'S HI-VIS SULPHUR EMERGER HAS TWO KEY ATTRIBUTES: it is very easy to see at the end of long casts, and it floats extremely well.

The slender silhouette makes the fly appear very natural on the surface of the water, and it is an excellent choice when trout are taking emergers in the slower sections of a stream. In addition to this sulphur version, tier Aaron Jasper makes this simple pattern in several sizes and colors to imitate almost any emerging mayfly he encounters while fishing.

If your local fly shop doesn't carry Z-Lon, which is used to make the fly's trailing shuck, simply substitute with Antron or polypropylene yarn.

Woodruff

Hook: Regular dry-fly hook, size 16 or 14.
Thread: White 8/0.
Tail: Light ginger hackle fibers.
Body: Light green or lime green dubbing.
Wings: Grizzly hackle tips.
Hackle: Light ginger.

THE WOODRUFF IS ANOTHER UNUSUAL PATTERN THAT shows an overlooked side of tying in the Catskill tradition: spinners.

The splayed, grizzly hackle tips mimic the wings of a spinner mayfly. In the coloration of this pattern, tied by David Brandt, the Woodruff imitates a sulphur mayfly.

Chester Mills, of the famed William Mills & Son sporting goods house in New York City, originated this pattern in 1920. He gave the fly to fishing friend John E. Woodruff, who tested it on the upper Beaverkill. When word spread of the great success he was having with the fly, anglers clamored to William Mills & Son to purchase the pattern. As a result, Mills named the fly in honor of Woodruff.

According to David Brandt, it is possible that the original Woodruff was tied with upright wings, but Harry Darbee tied the fly with spent or semi-spent wings. Harry routinely offered the fly to his customers in the 1930s and 1940s.

Emerger Callibaetis

Hook: Curved-shank emerger hook, sizes 18 to 14.
Thread: Gray 8/0.
Tail: Mottled hen-hackle fibers and gray or tan polypropylene yarn.
Abdomen: Pale yellow turkey biot.
Rib: Tan, small D-Rib.
Wing: Grizzly hen hackles tied in reverse.
Thorax: Light brown Superfine dubbing.
Hackle: Grizzly.

YOU CAN'T TIE A LOT OF MATERIALS ON A SMALL HOOK, but this Emerger Callibaetis, designed by Idaho's Todd Smith, has everything a fly needs to fool a trout.

The two-part tail, made using hen-hackle fibers and short strands of polypropylene yarn, simulates an emerging nymph just crawling out of its skin. The pattern has ample hackle fibers to keep the head of the fly above the water. And the wings, which are reversed, small-hen hackles, ideally imitate the wings of a real mayfly.

Come to think of it, if you work carefully and plan ahead, maybe you *can* tie a lot of stuff to a small hook.

Cross Special

Hook: Regular dry-fly hook, sizes 16 to 10.
Thread: Brown 8/0.
Tail: Blue dun.
Body: Light fox-belly fur.
Wing: Wood duck flank fibers.
Hackle: Blue dun.

THIS IS ONE MORE CLASSIC CATSKILL PATTERN. THE FAMED Rube Cross, a fly-tying legend in that part of the country, created this pattern.

I am including it because I want to share a rare tidbit about tying the Catskill family of patterns.

It's a little-known fact—only members of the Catskill Fly Tyers Guild and serious students of that style of tying know it—that you're supposed to leave a very small piece of bare shank between the hook eye and the thread head of the fly. The old-time tiers used this space for tying flies to their gut leaders with a turle knot. Theodore Gordon said that the turle knot was best for attaching a fly to the leader, and Rube Cross followed his example and left this small space on his flies. Walt Dette followed their lead and also left this tiny piece of bare shank.

Mike Valla, who learned to tie flies from the Dettes and dressed this example of the Cross Special, told me that story.

X2 Caddis

Hook: Regular dry-fly hook, size 14 or 12.
Thread: Brown 8/0.
Trailing shuck: Amber Zelon.
Body: Green hare's mask dubbing.
Underwing: White Widow's Web or Zelon.
Wing: Elk hair.
Head: Natural rabbit dubbing.

NO BOOK ABOUT FAVORITE TROUT FLIES WOULD BE COM-
plete without including a Craig Mathews pattern. Craig operates Blue Rib-
bon Flies, in West Yellowstone, Montana. He also created the X Caddis, a
fly sold commercially by Umpqua Feather Merchants. According to Bruce
Olson, who oversees the selection of new patterns included in the Umpqua
catalog, the X Caddis remains one of their best-selling flies. The X2 Caddis
is Craig's updated version of that original pattern.

In addition to being an experienced fly-shop owner, talented fly designer,
and crackerjack angler, Craig is also a leading conservationist. He was one
of the driving forces behind 1 Percent for the Planet. In this program, busi-
nesses pledge to contribute one percent of their net profits to their favorite
environmental causes. Many fly-fishing manufacturers and retailers partici-
pate in 1 Percent for the Planet.

In 2013, *Fly Tyer* magazine gave Craig its annual Lifetime Achievement
Award for being a leader in the fly fishing industry, a fly designer, and a
protector of the waters we all love to fish.

J:son Mayflies

Dun 1

Hook: Short-shank, wide-gap, light-wire hook, size 10 or 8.

Thread: Size 6/0.

Tails: Microfibbets or fibers from a synthetic paintbrush.

Abdomen: Closed-cell foam.

Hackle: Rooster.

Wings: J:son Realistic Wing Material.

LET'S CONSIDER THESE UNUSUAL PATTERNS, CREATED BY Claes Johansson of a Swedish company called J:son, as our challenge flies.

Yes, they are designed for fishing! They are very durable, and when you study them closely, you will see that they require very few materials; in fact, except for the wings, many other flies in this book are tied using the very same ingredients.

J:son specializes in innovative flies, fly-tying methods, and tying tools. Claes Johansson, the head of research and development at J:son (I don't know of another fly-tying company with a similarly named position), is always looking for ways to create realistic patterns designed for real-world fishing.

The flies in the accompanying photos are all tied using thread, closed-cell foam, hackles, and dubbing; you'll find any of these ingredients in your local fly shop. Claes fashions the wings using his company's sheet wing material, but you could couple one of his terrific-looking abdomens with a wing of elk hair, cul de canard, or your favorite material. (Go to www. jsonsweden.com to see full instructions on how to tie these flies and many more. It might revolutionize the way you think about pattern design.)

I'm including the recipe for the large mayfly imitation Claes calls Dun 1, as well as photos of his emerger and spinner imitations. When I asked him what it's supposed to imitate, he said, "I don't know; maybe a drake. What do you think?" Pinning him down is impossible. Claes is too inventive, and his mind is always working; I don't believe he thinks in terms of "patterns."

And that's why I'm including the flies of J:son in this little book. I don't know if they'll catch on and become an essential part of our fishing kits, but they do point to the need for tiers to keep experimenting. Innovation—exploring new materials, tools, methods, and patterns—keeps our fly-tying fresh and interesting.

CHAPTER TWO

The Overlooked Flies: Midges, Damselflies, and More

Hornberg

Hook: Tiemco TMC100, size 10.
Thread: Black 6/0.
Body: Flat silver tinsel.
Underwing: Yellow calf-tail hair.
Wings: Mallard-flank feathers.
Cheek: Jungle cock.
Hackle: Grizzly.

I DON'T KNOW WHEN THE HORNBERG BECAME KNOWN AS a streamer, but Col. Joseph Bates includes this pattern in his book, *Streamers and Bucktails: The Big Fish Flies.* Okay, that was Bates's opinion, but I use the Hornberg as a dry fly.

Actually, the Hornberg was created by Frank Hornberg, a game warden from central Wisconsin, in the 1920s. He called it the Hornberg Special and designed it to imitate a caddisfly.

The Hornberg (Sharon E. Wright tied this version) also works very well in late spring and early summer during a damselfly hatch. On my local Maine trout ponds, when the damselflies fly across the surface of the water, the trout rise quickly and sharp shoot these flitting insects. I cast the Hornberg several feet ahead of a cruising fish and slowly twitch the fly across the surface, imitating an egg-laying, female damselfly. The trout quickly responds.

Crane Fly

Hook: Regular dry-fly hook, size 16 or 14.
Thread: Pale yellow 6/0.
Abdomen: Pale yellow beaver dubbing.
Wings: Light dun hen-feather tips.
Wing post: Gray McFlylon.
Thorax and legs: Ginger cul de canard.
Hackle: Light ginger.

CRANE FLY IMITATIONS ARE ONE OF THE MOST OVER-
looked group of patterns. Make no mistake, however, that the trout do feed
on these gangly looking insects.

Crane flies have very long legs and long, slender abdomens. Unlike most
insects, crane flies are poor fliers with a tendency to wobble in unpredict-
able patterns during flight. You'll often see them hovering over the water,
looking a little lost and flying without purpose. Adult crane flies feed on
nectar, or they do not feed at all; most species of crane flies exist only to
mate and then die.

North America has more than 500 species of crane flies, so you can bet
you will encounter these insects on your local trout stream.

Tie the hen-hackle-tip wings splayed along the top of the back. Tier
Dennis Charney makes the thorax and legs using cul de canard. The CDC
increases the buoyancy of the pattern, and according to Dennis, "Does a
great job imitating the spindly legs of the natural insect."

I.C.S.I. (I Can See It) Midge

Hook: Curved-shank emerger hook, size 20 or 18.
Thread: Golden olive 6/0.
Wing post: Fluorescent orange yarn.
Hackle: Grizzly.
Body: Muskrat-belly fur (in this fly, trapped on the Letort by Ed Shenk), finely spun onto thread.

THE I.C.S.I. (I CAN SEE IT) MIDGE SUGGESTS A NYMPH OR pupa just under the water surface and is particularly useful during any emergence of small mayflies, midges, and even tiny caddisflies on both lakes and rivers. Its origin predates similar-looking European patterns, and it has been a best-selling small dry fly in the Orvis catalog for many years.

A black-bodied version, designed to imitate a dark midge, has proven quite effective during *trico* spinner falls. Try other colors, too. The suggestion of a nymph or pupa stuck under the surface film holds a powerful attraction to trout. The first time this fly hit the water, a trout rose and sucked it in.

The post material on this pattern is a fiber-optic, synthetic yarn. Tie it onto the underside of the hook shank, pull the ends up each side of the shank, and post it with a couple of wraps of thread. Trim the post to length after wrapping the hackle.

Foam Damselfly

Hook: Regular dry-fly hook, size 12.
Thread: Blue or black 8/0.
Abdomen: Blue closed-cell foam damselfly body.
Thorax: Blue dubbing.
Wings: White polypropylene yarn.
Hackle: Grizzly, dyed blue.

DAMSELFLIES BEGIN EMERGING IN JUNE AND ARE PRESENT throughout the summer; you'll see them flying fast and low over the water. If you fish trout ponds, you'll often have damselflies land on your rod, line, and float tube. You'll often see male and female damselflies connected together while mating.

A good damselfly hatch is a memorable event; dozens of the large insects will be present on the water. Fishing a damselfly imitation, such as this simple Foam Damselfly, is also a unique event; it will be one of the largest dry flies you will cast during the season.

Even though a damselfly pattern is large, it does not have to be heavy. My Foam Damselfly is extremely lightweight; I regularly fish it using a four-weight rod and 5X leader. Spread a small drop of cement on each wing to stiffen the fibers; this prevents the wings from fouling around the hook when casting.

Black Gnat Snowshoe

Hook: Regular dry-fly hook, size 18 or 16.
Thread: Black 8/0.
Tail: Black snowshoe hare foot fur.
Body: Black snowshoe hare foot fur.
Wing: White or bleached snowshoe hare foot fur.
Hackle: Black.

SHOW ME A PIECE OF TROUT WATER THAT DOESN'T HAVE its share of little black insects flittering across the surface, and I'll show you a stream not worth fishing.

Whether they are small stoneflies, gnats, or midges, at some time or another, there will be a hatch of some sort of very small, black insect. And fortunately, as the insects get smaller in size, you can get away with using less precise imitations. Typically, you'll simply need a pattern that matches the size of the natural and makes a realistic impression on the surface of the water. The Black Gnat Snowshoe is the sort of diminutive fly that matches several types of insects.

Use this pattern when real gnats and midges are on the water. This is also a fine choice for when the small, black stoneflies are laying eggs; this often happens on balmy, late winter and early spring days, and it can result in some of the first rises of trout for the season.

Griffith's Gnat

Hook: Regular dry-fly hook, sizes 24 to 18.
Thread: Black 8/0.
Body: Peacock herl.
Hackle: Grizzly.

DO YOU NEED A SMALL DRY? I MEAN, A PATTERN SO SMALL it's almost impossible to get the materials onto the diminutive hook? Then the Griffith's Gnat might be the answer.

When tying a midge imitation, there is no reason to struggle making an exact imitation; the fish won't be able to perceive all those complicated parts. At most, the pattern should match the size of the natural insects and imitate the dimpling of the legs in the surface film. These are the two key features of the Griffith's Gnat.

George Griffith, one of the founders of Trout Unlimited, created the famed Griffith's Gnat. One evening, while fishing the Benedict's Crossing section of Vermont's Batten Kill River, the trout were rising to impossibly small midges. I tried several small patterns with no success. I rummaged through my vest and found a lonely Griffith's Gnat. I knotted the fly to the end of my 7X tippet and caught several Batten Kill brown trout.

Thank you, Mr. Griffith!

Tying the Griffith's Gnat

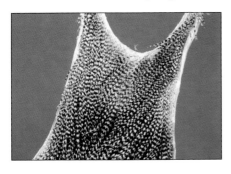

1. The tiny hackles at the base of a dry-fly cape are perfect for fashioning diminutive midge imitations such as the Griffith's Gnat.

2. Tie a hackle and piece of peacock herl to the hook.

3. Wrap the herl up the hook to form the body of the fly. Tie off and clip the remaining piece of herl.

4. Spiral wrap the hackle over the body. Tie off and cut the excess hackle tip. Whip finish and snip the thread.

CHAPTER THREE

Important Terrestrials: Inchworms, Grasshoppers, and Ants

Hot Legs Hopper

Hook: Regular dry-fly hook, size 8.
Thread: Tan 6/0.
Body: Yellow closed-cell foam colored with black permanent marker.
Rear legs: Hopper legs.
Front legs: Rubber legs.
Antennae: Extra-fine rubber legs.
Wing: Brown Bugskin.
Indicator: Pink polypropylene yarn.

CHUCK FURIMSKY, A LONGTIME FRIEND, DESIGNED THE Hot Legs Hopper. Chuck founded the annual International Fly Tying Symposium more than twenty years ago, and he is the promoter of the national string of fly-fishing carnivals called The Fly Fishing Show. Through these efforts, I believe Chuck has done more than almost anyone to educate the public about fly fishing and tying; every year, thousands of expert anglers, as well as people who have never cast a rod or caught a fish, come to his shows to improve their casting, discover new places to fish, and learn a few fly-tying tricks.

Chuck has also run a successful leather-goods business, and he markets a leather fly-tying material called Bugskin. He uses brown Bugskin to fashion the wing on his Hot Legs Hopper.

Letort Hopper

Hook: 3X-long, dry-fly hook, sizes 18 to 10.
Thread: Yellow 8/0.
Body: Pale yellow superfine dubbing.
Underwing: Mottled turkey-wing quill.
Wing: Natural deer hair.

WHO SAYS A GRASSHOPPER IMITATION HAS TO BE COMPLI-cated? The Letort Hopper, created by Ed Shenk more than fifty years ago, is still a go-to pattern for many knowledgeable anglers.

Ed says he got the idea for this pattern while fishing Muddler Minnows as grasshopper imitations. Those flies, normally fished as streamers, caught trout. Shenk thought that a similar fly, substituting yellow dubbing for the gold-tinsel body, would work even better. He called it the Letort Hopper.

The Letort Hopper is a simple, streamlined pattern. Even without the usual grasshopper legs, it creates the right silhouette on the water and fools trout. The Letort Hopper is a great grasshopper imitation for new tiers who find more complicated flies too difficult to tie. And the Letort Hopper catches fish wherever fish eat grasshoppers. It is a fine addition to your summer fly-fishing kit.

I.C.S.I. (I Can See It) Ant

Hook: Regular dry-fly hook, size 16 or 14.
Thread: Black 6/0.
Post: Fluorescent orange or lemon yellow calf-body hair.
Hackle: Grizzly.
Body: Black or brown rabbit-fur dubbing.

THE I.C.S.I. (I CAN SEE IT) ANT RANKS THIRD ON TOM BALTZ'S list of top-three dry flies. This current version is an evolution of a design the late Dr. Jack Beck, of Carlisle, Pennsylvania, gave to him.

During midday, when the hatches of aquatic insects lag, is a good time to try an ant imitation. Ants are ubiquitous and found anywhere a trout might live. Few bugs hold a more powerful attraction for trout during the temperate months from late March through November.

Fish your ant along the banks of large rivers and anywhere in medium- to smaller-sized streams. Orange or yellow wing posts are useful depending upon lighting conditions. This parachute ant also doubles nicely for a flying ant.

Wrap the hackle counter clockwise and tie it off on the side of the hook shank in front of the post. Try placing the post just in front of the midpoint of the hook shank. Spin the dubbing tightly on the thread and build the body "humps" in three layers.

Parachute Ant

Hook: Regular dry-fly hook, size 14.
Thread: Black 8/0.
Body: Black dry-fly dubbing.
Hackle: Black.
Wing bud: White polypropylene yarn.

IN SOME PARTS OF THE COUNTRY, ESPECIALLY DURING late summer, ants become an important source of food for the trout. This is when you will want to have a small collection of ant imitations in your fishing kit.

Gary Borger prefers fishing with this unique Parachute Ant. In addition to the parachute hackle wrapped around the front section of the body, he adds a tiny wing bud of polypropylene yarn; you can see it peeking out of the bottom of the fly.

Sometimes ants fall onto the water and are available to the trout. Pay attention, however, for flights of ants. Some of the insects crash onto the water and will turn on the fish. Use a long, light leader, and tie on the Parachute Ant or one of the other imitations in this book. You will enjoy some memorable fishing to a unique form of "hatch."

70

Potter's Fat Head Moth

Hook: Tiemco TMC100, size 12 or 10.
Thread: Fifty denier, gel-spun thread.
Abdomen: Tan or cinnamon Superfine dubbing.
Rib: Opal Mirage tinsel.
Head and wing: Natural, dark elk hair.

DO YOU HAVE ANY MOTH IMITATIONS IN YOUR FLY BOX? IF not, then you might be missing out on some good fishing.

Moths and butterflies inhabit the riverbank from mid to late summer. Occasionally, one of these insects haphazardly lands on the water. Struggling to free itself and regain the air, it will attract the attention of the trout. Keep watching, and you might see a fish snatch this morsel.

Dennis Potter uses his Fat Head Moth from dusk until after dark from late June into August. He says this is a big-fish pattern. It certainly is an unusual terrestrial imitation that will bring a new, refreshing dimension to your fly fishing.

Grand Hopper

Hook: 2X-long dry-fly hook, size 8.
Thread: Tan 6/0.
Body: Closed-cell foam colored with permanent marker.
Underwing: Pearl Krystal Flash.
Wing: Tan feather placed on tape and clipped to shape. Add spots using a permanent marker.
Legs: Rubber legs.
Collar: Tan dubbing.
Eyes: Black pinheads.

GRASSHOPPERS INHABIT THE BANKS OF MANY RIVERS from the East to West Coasts during late summer and early autumn, and imitations of these important terrestrials populate the fly boxes of many anglers during this time of the season.

Many popular grasshopper patterns are tied using only hair and feathers, but they eventually become waterlogged and sink. With the acceptance of closed-cell foam as a fly-tying material, it is possible to create a grasshopper, and other patterns, that float forever.

Rainy's Grand Hopper is ideal for fishing wherever trout feed on hapless grasshoppers that fall or fly onto the water. Change body colors to create imitations of any grasshopper you find along the river.

Harvey Deer-hair Inchworm

Hook: 3X-long dry-fly hook, sizes 16 to 10.
Thread: Green 6/0.
Body: Bright green deer hair.

GEORGE HARVEY WAS ONE OF THE GREATEST ANGLERS OF the twentieth century. I was pleased to meet this angling legend at the International Fly Tying Symposium. Mr. Harvey developed many fish-catching patterns, and his Deer-hair Inchworm is one of his most unusual.

Many anglers have reported times when real inchworms were falling into the water and sending trout into feeding frenzies; the fish quickly catch on that the unprotected worms are something good to eat. Curiously, Harvey's solution to the inchworm-fishing challenge was to create a fly using only spun-and-clipped deer hair. Does it look like an inchworm? Maybe not, but the trout do like it.

Ed Shenk, who wrote about this fly when describing his favorite terrestrial imitations, recommends tying the Harvey Deer-hair Inchworm using bright green hair.

CDC Foam Ant

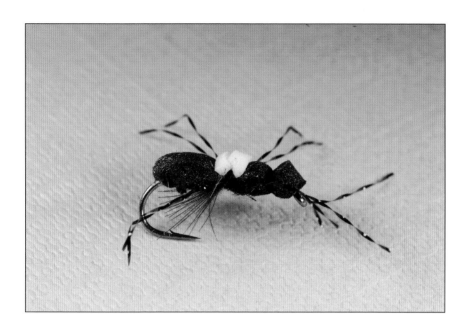

Hook: Regular dry-fly hook, sizes 18 to 12.
Thread: Size 6/0.
Body: Closed-cell foam.
Throat: Cul de canard.
Indicator: Yellow closed-cell foam.
Legs and antennae: Crystal Splash.

THE CDC FOAM ANT IS AN INTERESTING TAKE ON A common ant imitation. Fly bins across the country contain foam-bodied ant patterns, but the Spirit River Company has made a couple of additions you might want to consider for the ants you tie.

First, the throat of cul de canard improves the floatation of a foam-bodied pattern that is already unsinkable. The CDC helps the fly float a little higher than a standard ant pattern.

The legs and antennae, tied using Crystal Splash (you may substitute with Krystal Flash), is a worthwhile change. These appendages are easy to make, and they do not weigh the fly down.

Other than the yellow foam indicator, the pattern recipe specifies no colors. You might, however, encounter black or red ants, so choose materials in colors to imitate these common ants. And if you need some flying ants, simply tie your favorite wing material to the top of the pattern before adding the foam indicator.

Hyper Hopper

Extended body

Base: Flymen Fishing Company Wiggle Shank.

Thread: Hopper yellow 8/0.

Egg sac: Fluorescent orange Gator Hair.

Abdomen: Tan closed-cell foam.

Thorax

Hook: Daiichi 1280 or 1710, sizes 14 to 10.

Thread: Hopper yellow 8/0.

Extended-body connection: 4X fluorocarbon tippet.

Thorax: Tan closed-cell foam.

Legs: Rubber legs.

Underwing: Opal Mirage Flash.

Wing: Dark tan Widow's Web.

Hot spot: Fluorescent-orange Gator Hair.

AL RITT PULLED OUT ALL THE STOPS WHEN DESIGNING this fun grasshopper imitation. Still, if you study the Hyper Hopper closely, you'll see that any tier with moderate skills can make it.

Al tied the extended abdomen of the fly on a Wiggle Shank, a product of the Flymen Fishing Company. He attached the abdomen to the hook shank using 4X-tippet material before making the front section of the fly.

Al fashions the grasshopper's legs using rubber leg material. A piece of tan rubber leg makes the fly's two front legs. Each thigh of the back legs are three strands of rubber leg material left together. Al carefully glues a piece of small Centipede Legs to the end of the thigh to create an ankle.

The closed-cell foam body floats forever, and the synthetic wing dries with one or two false casts. This pattern will not sink even after catching several trout.

Letort Cricket

Hook: 3X-long dry-fly hook, sizes 18 to 10.
Thread: Black 8/0.
Body: Black Superfine dubbing.
Underwing: Black goose- or turkey-wing quill.
Wing: Black deer hair.

ED SHENK SAYS HE TIED THE LETORT CRICKET A COUPLE OF years after creating the Letort Hopper. He got the idea for his cricket imitation while watching that storied stream's trophy trout eating crickets and refusing his grasshopper. Although the patterns are similar in design, the Letort Cricket is black.

In some ways, the Letort Cricket has been more successful than the Letort Hopper. Ed says he caught a three-and-a-half-pound trout the first time he used the new fly. He also caught a Letort trout that measured twenty-seven and one-quarter inches long and, he estimates, weighed close to nine pounds using this pattern; that was the largest trout Shenk has caught on the Letort using a dry fly.

It's always more fun catching fish using your own flies.

Mr. Bill's Fly Ant

Hook: Regular dry-fly hook, sizes 18 to 10.
Thread: Size 6/0.
Body: Antron dubbing.
Wing: Wings & Things.
Legs and antennae: Crystal Splash.

SWARMS OF FLYING ANTS ARE PART OF THE MATING ritual of ants. Although the majority of winged ants are males, a few females are mixed into the swarm. If they survive, these females will become future queens and perhaps establish new colonies.

City and suburban dwellers fear the sight of flying ants because it's a sign that new colonies may be established, perhaps in their homes or apartments. For fly fishermen, however, flying ants are the sign of potentially good angling. Ants aren't born fliers, and some will crash into nearby streams and encourage the trout to feed. This happens during the heat of summer.

Mr. Bill's Fly Ant is a good, simple imitation of a winged ant. The legs, tied using Crystal Splash (you may substitute with Krystal Flash), splay on the water like the real insect. The simple wing is made using a material called Wings & Things (Medallion Sheeting is a suitable substitute).

Tie the Mr. Bill's Flying Ant in black and cinnamon to match the winged ants you find along your local trout stream.

Jassid

Hook: Regular dry-fly hook, sizes 24 to 16.
Thread: Black 8/0.
Body: Tying thread.
Hackle: Black.
Wing: Jungle-cock nail.

ED SHENK IS ONE OF THE LAST OF THAT FAMOUS GROUP OF anglers who raised the bar in American fly fishing in the middle of the twentieth century. Based in central Pennsylvania, Shenk, George Harvey, Charlie Fox, Vince Marinaro, Joe Humphrey, and their friends closely studied the trout living in the nearby limestone streams, and they designed imitations of the local insects. They wrote about their observations and findings and revolutionized the concept of match the hatch.

The Jassid is one of the unusual patterns that came out of their work. It was first covered in an article that appeared in *Outdoor Life* magazine in 1958. The Jassid is designed to imitate a leafhopper and is particularly effective during hot weather when the stream-bank foliage is full of these insects.

Add a drop of cement to the wing to prevent the jungle-cock feather from splitting when fishing the fly.

CHAPTER FOUR

Attractor Patterns: The Anti-imitators

Royal Wulff

Hook: 2X-long dry-fly hook, sizes 18 to 8. (The fly shown in the photograph was dressed on an Atlantic salmon dry-fly hook.)

Thread: Black 8/0 (Seventy denier).

Tail: Brown bucktail.

Body: Peacock herl and red floss.

Wing: White bucktail.

Hackle: Brown.

NO BOOK ABOUT FAVORITE DRY FLIES WOULD BE COM-plete without the venerable Royal Wulff. This is undoubtedly the most famous pattern created by the late Lee Wulff. Although he originally tied this fly to fish for sea-run Atlantic salmon—yes, they really do snatch dry flies from the surface of the water—the Royal Wulff has since been called the unofficial state bird of Montana. All coldwater fish—trout, salmon, gray-ling, and more—will strike a high-floating Royal Wulff.

Built with the body of a Royal Coachman, the Royal Wulff has two outstanding characteristics: a thick-hair wing and a bushy-hackle collar. The wing makes the fly easy to spot on the water, and the hackle keeps the fly afloat. These two features also make the pattern challenging to make.

Select fine bucktail when tying the wings on large Royal Wulffs. Some tiers use calf-tail hair when making smaller versions of this pattern, but these hairs are usually thick and slightly curled. Fine goat hair is a better option for making the wings on small Royal Wulffs.

Use two or even three hackles for making the thick collar. Another option is to use one of the extra-long saddle dry-fly hackles. Simply tie the feather to the hook and make as many wraps as you wish to create the heavy collar.

The Royal Wulff you see here, which was loaned to me by Lee's good friend Ted Rogowski, was actually tied by Lee Wulff.

Ausable Wulff

Hook: Regular dry-fly hook, sizes 16 to 12.
Thread: Fluorescent orange 6/0.
Tail: Woodchuck-guard hair.
Body: Rusty orange, Australian opossum fur.
Wing: Calf-tail or calf-body hair.
Hackle: Cree, or grizzly and brown hackles.

YOU'RE ALREADY FAMILIAR WITH THE WULFF SERIES OF dry flies. Lee Wulff originally created these heavily hackled patterns for catching Atlantic salmon, but other anglers quickly downsized them to fish for trout. Fran Betters, a leading fly designer from New York's Adirondack Mountains, used Lee's formula—a thick tail, easy-to-see wing, and bushy hackle—to develop the Ausable Wulff.

The Ausable River, which flows through the Adirondacks, is a favorite destination for eastern trout anglers. The green drake hatch is one of the most important hatches on the river. The Ausable Wulff is great for matching a green drake; the body color might not be an exact match, but the size of this pattern attracts the fish.

The green drake hatch generally occurs during the first two weeks of June. Be sure to linger on the river until early evening for the spinner fall. During the spinner fall, the river seems to come alive with fish rising until well after dark. Continue casting your Ausable Wulff, and you will have a good chance of catching a trophy.

Quick 'n EZY Double Magic

Hook: Regular dry-fly hook, sizes 22 to 10.
Thread: Tan 8/0.
Tail: Ginger hackle fibers.
Body: Ginger dubbing.
Rib: Tying thread.
Wings: Ginger hackles.
Hackle: Ginger.

AL AND GRETCHEN BEATTY, OF BOISE, IDAHO, TIED THIS PAT-
tern called the Quick 'n EZY Double Magic. It features their technique
called Wonder Wings.

Wonder Wings are two hackles tied on in reverse. The fibers mimic the
veins in a mayfly wing. Wonder Wings create the silhouette of a real mayfly's
wings. The Beattys also make a caddisfly imitation with one Wonder Wing
tied flat over the back of the pattern.

Except for the Wonder Wings, I can almost see the influence of the
Catskill school of tying in the Quick 'n EZY Double Magic. The delicate,
slender body and perfect hackle remind me of many of those classic patterns; the wings, however, speak to the influence of more modern Western
tying techniques.

81

The Usual

Hook: Standard dry-fly hook, sizes 20 to 12.
Thread: Hot orange 6/0 (140 denier).
Tail, wing, and body: Natural snowshoe hare fur from the underside of the paw.

FRAN BETTERS WAS A LEGEND ALONG THE BANKS OF NEW York's Au Sable River. He opened one of the first fly shops in the United States, and he developed many great patterns. All knowledgeable anglers visiting the Adirondacks would stop to meet and chat with Fran at his Adirondack Sports Shop. I visited Fran's shop several times, and he was always sitting in a rocking chair behind the counter, his vise perched in his lap, tying flies. He was quick to share tips, discuss recent hatches, and relay fishing reports. Fran was inducted into the Fly Fishing Hall of Fame in 2008, and he passed away shortly after that.

Fran was not a "neat" tier; his flies typically had a disheveled appearance. Fran's patterns require few materials, and tiers with only modest skills can master his flies. The Usual is one of Fran's most enduring creations. It was originally designed as a general imitation of a Hendrickson mayfly, and you can select hook sizes and colors of materials to tie imitations of other mayflies.

Perhaps "materials" is too strong a word when describing the components of The Usual. This simple pattern requires only three ingredients: a hook, a spool of thread, and the fur from the foot of a snowshoe hare.

Snowshoe hare foot fur is curly and traps small air bubbles that keep The Usual afloat. Since the introduction of this pattern, other tiers have designed dry flies featuring this translucent and durable ingredient. Do not, however, become discouraged with the appearance of the flies you tie using this corkscrewed hair; they will look a little messy. The Usual, however, does catch a lot of trout.

Tying The Usual

1. Start the thread on the hook. Wrap a thread base on the shank. Clip a small bunch of fur from a snowshoe hare foot. Strip the underfur from the base of the bunch and set aside; we'll use it in a moment to complete the fly. Next, tie the bunch to the top of the hook with the tips pointing forward. Clip the butt ends at an angle and cover with firm wraps of thread.

2. Clip a smaller bunch of hair from the foot. Strip the underfur from the base of the bunch and set aside. Tie the hair to the end of the hook shank to make the tail of the fly.

3. Smear dubbing wax on the thread. Spin the underfur on the thread and twist into a noodle. Wrap the dubbing up the hook to create the body of the fly. Make a wrap of dubbing in front of the hair wing. Tie off the thread and clip. The thread commonly shows through the body of The Usual. This is not considered a polished pattern, but it does catch trout.

The Coyote

Hook: Partridge Bomber hook, size 2.
Thread: Brown 3/0.
Tail: Deer hair.
Body: Spun-and-clipped deer hair.
Hackle: Brown.
Wing: Deer hair.

WARREN DUNCAN, WHO CAME FROM NEW BRUNSWICK, Canada, remains a recognized leader in tying hair-wing Atlantic salmon flies. The Picture Province, which is the official fly of New Brunswick, and the Undertaker are two of his personal patterns.

This beautifully tied fly is called the Coyote. Although Warren made it for catching salmon, like the Royal Wulff, you can downsize it for trout fishing. In fact, the Wulff series of flies gave Warren the idea for the name of this pattern.

One day, while I was visiting his fly shop, called Dunc's, in Saint John, New Brunswick, Warren handed me a card with several of his flies pinned around the edges. Warren pointed to one of the flies and said, "See that one? That's the Coyote. There's a Wulff, so that's the Coyote. Get it?" With that he gave one of his hearty laughs that we all miss so much.

This is the first time the Coyote has appeared in print. And, just for fun, I am including a picture of Warren's take on the Royal Wulff; I believe this is another of his flies that has never been shown in a book or magazine.

Spirit of Harford Mills

Hook: Regular dry-fly hook, size 12.
Thread: Brown 8/0.
Tail: Badger-guard hairs.
Body: Light, dyed-olive rabbit fur and ginger hackle.
Wing: Grizzly rooster-hackle tips.
Hackle: Golden badger.

MIKE VALLA CREATED THE SPIRIT OF HARFORD MILLS circa 1975. The famous Spirit of Pittsford Mills dry fly, created by Stephen Belcher II, of Vermont, inspired it. Belcher's pattern, tied by Elsie Darbee, was featured in the color plates in A.J. McClane's book, *Fisherman's Encyclopedia*, where Mike first noticed it.

The Spirit of Harford Mills is named for the hamlet of Harford Mills, along Owego Creek in central New York State. The Owego was one of his favorite haunts; he had fished there since he was a boy. When Mike attended Cornell University—more years ago than he cares to admit—he would ride a bike to there from campus.

It is great to see the classic, Catskill style of pattern still used to commemorate contemporary thoughts and emotions.

Grizzly Wulff

Hook: 2X-long dry-fly hook, sizes 18 to 8. (The fly shown in the photograph was dressed on an Atlantic salmon dry-fly hook.)
Thread: Black 8/0 (seventy denier).
Tail: Brown bucktail.
Body: Green, wool yarn.
Wing: Brown bucktail.
Hackle: Grizzly.

LEE WULFF TIED THIS EXAMPLE OF THE GRIZZLY WULFF. LEE did not tie flies with the aid of a vise; he actually held the hook between the fingers of one hand and applied materials using his other hand. While it's relatively easy to understand wrapping thread, yarn, tinsel, and similar materials around a hook shank, imagine the challenges of mounting wing and tail materials. Try it sometime; it's quite a naughty problem.

Lee tied the Grizzly Wulff shown in the photograph for fishing for Altantic salmon, but you can make trout-size Grizzly Wulffs using smaller hooks. You can make the body of the Grizzly Wulff using green wool yarn as shown, substitute with another color, or use dubbing.

A lot of tiers run out of room on the hook when tying a Wulff pattern—the wing and bushy hackle take up a lot of space—but this problem is easy to solve. Divide the hook into two parts when tying a Wulff. The first half, which requires absolutely no more than two-thirds (or less) of the hook shank, contains the body of the fly. Wrap the hackle, which is the second major part of the fly, on the remaining one-third of the shank. Pay attention to these dimensions, and you will have ample room on the hook shank to tie the fly.

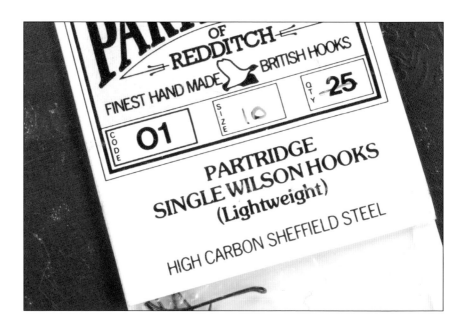

Egg-sucking Gnat

Hook: Daiichi 1280, sizes 12 to 8.
Thread: Orange 6/0.
Body: Peacock herl.
Rib: Grizzly dry-fly hackle.
Wing and head: Fluorescent orange deer hair.
Legs: Yellow and black rubber legs.

TIED ON 2X-LONG HOOKS, IN SIZES 12 TO 8, THE EGG-SUCK-
ing Gnat doesn't remind me of a diminutive gnat. Colorado fly-tier Al Ritt
created this fly as an attractor pattern.

Al is a guide who works the water flowing out of Rocky Mountain
National Park. While he and his clients do encounter the local hatches,
there are times when there is no insect activity, and they cast attractors to
catch the resident trout. The Egg-sucking Gnat is a buggy-looking, easy-to-
see fly that maintains its balance on the clear, flowing mountain water. The
splayed rubber legs, spiral-wrapped hackle, and wing suggest—but do not
exactly imitate—a stonefly or other large insect on the water.

86

Bomber

Hook: 2X-long dry-fly hook, sizes 16 to 12.
Thread: Size 8/0, color to match the body.
Tail: Deer hair.
Body: Rabbit dubbing.
Wing: Deer hair.
Note: Select materials in your choice of colors. Fran Betters dressed the Bomber *in white, brown, olive, and black.*

THIS PATTERN MIGHT BE FRAN BETTERS'S ANSWER TO THE Bomber tied for catching Atlantic salmon. Whereas the salmon Bomber has a complicated, spun-and-clipped deer hair body, Fran used dubbing to tie the body on his fly.

Like most of Fran's flies, his Bombers are a little scruffy, but they do catch fish. The Bomber is great for skating across the surface of the water and will generate explosive rises from trout and landlocked salmon.

These two flies were from an article Fran wrote about the Bomber for *Fly Tyer* magazine many years ago; he submitted these samples for the photography appearing with that piece. Although he preferred using more subdued colors, you can select bright colors for the wing—pink or hot orange—to increase the pattern's visibility in low-light conditions.

Bi-visible

Hook: 3X-long dry-fly hook, sizes 16 to 6.
Thread: White 8/0.
Tail: Three hackle tips.
Body: Three brown hackles.
Face: White or cream hackle.

THE BI-VISIBLE PROVES A THEORY I'VE HELD ABOUT DRY flies for many years. Fancy wings and other do–dads that remain above the water are designed to catch fishermen; the gentle dimpling of hackle tips and tail materials in the surface attract the trout.

The Bi-visible matches no insect yet imitates many. Perhaps the fish mistake it for a mayfly, caddisfly, damselfly, or some other insect. Who cares? It is what we consider an attractor pattern, and it does attract trout.

With respect to making the Bi-visible, one author pegs the degree of difficulty at level four, but he mustn't have much experience at the tying bench. The Bi-visible is a fairly straightforward pattern. Follow the accompanying tying instructions, and you'll quickly turn out fine Bi-visibles that will catch fish on your local waters.

Just a note before we tie the fly: some tiers include the tail in the Bi-visible, and others do not. I am adding the tail to match the fly in the main photograph.

Tying the Bi-visible

1. Wrap a layer of thread on the hook shank. Stack three hackles with the tips even. Measure from the tips to the spot where you will tie the feathers to the hook to create the tail; I like the length of the tail to equal to overall length of the hook. Brush the hackle fibers toward the base to expose the bare stems. Tie the feathers to the hook to make the tail.

2. Hold the hackle toward the end of the fly. Wrap one of the feathers two-thirds of the way up the shank. Tie off and clip the remaining piece of hackle.

3. Wrap the remaining two hackles—one at a time—two-thirds of the way up the hook. Rock each feather back and forth while working to prevent binding down the fibers of the previously wrapped feathers. Tie off and cut the excess pieces of hackle.

4. Tie a white or cream hackle in front of the body.

5. Wrap the face of the fly. Tie off and cut the surplus piece of feather. Whip finish and snip the thread.

Opal Wulff

Hook: Tiemco TMC100, size 12 or 10.
Thread: Fifty denier, gel-spun thread.
Tail: Moose-body hair.
Body: Opal Mirage tinsel.
Wing: Light gray EP Fibers or an equivalent.
Hackle: Brown.

DENNIS POTTER HAS ALTERED SEVERAL VENERABLE WULFF
patterns, updating them with his own methods. For example, he substituted
a synthetic wing for the standard-hair wing on this Wulff; Dennis used EP
Fibers, which are usually considered a saltwater tying material, but you can
use the ingredient of your choice. The wing holds its shape and has a great
silhouette. And rather than dubbing, or the famous peacock herl and red
floss found on the Royal Wulff, Dennis uses opal tinsel.

Wulff flies are usually used as attractor patterns, and the Opal Wulff fits
right in. It is a great selection for fishing broken currents and pocket water.

Wemoc Adams

Hook: Regular dry-fly hook, size 12.
Thread: Brown 8/0.
Tail: Cree hackle fibers.
Body: Muskrat-fur dubbing.
Rib: Fine, gold wire.
Wing: Grizzly rooster-hackle tips.
Hackle: Cree.

THE WEMOC ADAMS, CREATED IN THE LATE 1970S AFTER fishing it on Willowemoc Creek in the Catskills, is Mike Valla's tweak of the common Adams dry fly. Mike does not claim that this fly is an entirely new concept. However, he uses what Eric Leiser used to call "Adams hackle," which is Cree. He adds fine, gold wire as a rib to help the muskrat-fur dubbing stay in place when fishing.

The fly was first featured in Mike's great book, *Tying Catskill Style Dry Flies,* and in his *Classic Dry Fly Box*; I have both well-thumbed volumes in my library.

Interestingly, Anne Lively, daughter of the late fly-tier Chauncy K. Lively, made a watercolor painting of the Wemoc Adams. Fly tying is a form of art, and it inspires art!

Searcher

Hook: Regular dry-fly hook, size 14.
Thread: Black 8/0.
Tail: Golden pheasant-tibbet fibers.
Tag: Red floss.
Body: Tying thread.
Wing: White or bleached snowshoe hare foot fur.

MOST PATTERNS TIED USING SNOWSHOE HARE FOOT FUR have a ragged, scruffy appearance. The material is unruly, so fly designers throw in the towel and use it to create disheveled-looking patterns. Ken Walrath's fly, the Searcher, is a pleasant surprise.

The Searcher has a trim tail, colorful butt, neat body, and perfectly wrapped hackle. The bright wings, made using snowshoe hare foot fur, are easy to spot on the water. Except for the wings, you might think this pattern came out of the Catskill tradition of fly tying.

As the name implies, this fly imitates no specific insect. Ken uses it as a general-searching pattern for exploring pocket water and other likely lies.

Crystal Wing Royal Wulff
Hook: 2X-long dry-fly hook, sizes 18 to 12.
Thread: Red 6/0.
Tail: Elk hair.
Body: Peacock herl and red floss.
Wings: Crystal Splash.
Hackle: Dark brown.

Crystal Wing Gray Wulff
Hook: 2X-long dry-fly hook, sizes 18 to 12.
Thread: Gray 6/0.
Tail: Elk hair.
Body: Gray floss.
Wing: Crystal Splash.
Hackle: Medium dun.

THE WULFF SERIES OF FLIES, CREATED BY LEE WULFF, ARE some of our most popular patterns. Unfortunately, they are also a tad difficult to make; they're not the place to begin if you are a new fly tier. The bushy wings create bulk in the bodies, and tying the full-hackle collars is challenging. These versions of the Royal Wulff and Gray Wulff, sporting wings of a material called Crystal Splash, are easier to tie. The wings create less bulk on the hooks and leave more room for wrapping the hackle collars. If your local fly shop doesn't stock Crystal Splash, a product of the Spirit River Company, you can substitute with Krystal Flash.

CRYSTAL WING ROYAL WULFF

CRYSTAL WING GRAY WULFF

B.G. Dun

Hook: Regular dry-fly hook, sizes 16 to 12.
Thread: Gray 8/0.
Tail: Light dun hackle fibers.
Body: Stripped dun hackle quill.
Wings: Wood duck flank fibers.
Hackle: Grizzly and dun.

LEGENDARY FLY TIER AND GOOD FRIEND DAVID BRANDT
originated the B.G. Dun. (I call him "legendary" because it will embarrass
him.) "B.G.," he says, "is short for my pen name, Brooks Gordon—even
though I don't have a pen yet."

According to David, the B.G. Dun represents no specific insect, yet it
imitates many. He ties the fly in a range of sizes and shades. And although
he prefers using real wood duck flank feathers for the wings, he has no
objection to using mallard flank. With respect to using dyed mallard as a
substitute, however, he says, "I don't like dyed mallard feathers because they
don't feel the same as real wood duck."

Although this is a modern creation, the B.G. Dun is tied in the Catskill
tradition.

Opal Trude

Hook: Tiemco TMC2312, sizes 16 to 10.
Thread: Red 8/0.
Abdomen: Opal Mirage tinsel.
Rib: Fine, gold wire.
Thorax: Peacock herl or peacock Arizona Synthetic Dubbing.
Wing: Light gray EP Fibers or an equivalent.
Hackle: Brown.

DENNIS POTTER, WHO OPERATES THE RIVERHOUSE FLY Company on the banks of Michigan's Ausable River, borrowed the Trude moniker for this pattern years ago; he was tying Trudes back then and got stuck looking for a name. It is mildly reminiscent of the hair-wing Trudes that were developed for use on the Henry's Fork water of the Snake River in Idaho.

This is another of Dennis's dry flies that use opal tinsel for the body. Even though this pattern rides high and dry, Dennis insists that the tinsel increases the fish-attracting properties of the pattern.

Grumpy Frumpy

Hook: 2X-long dry-fly hook, size 12
Thread: Red 8/0.
Tail: Brown polypropylene yarn.
Body: Yellow floss.
Back: Tan closed-cell foam.
Legs: Rubber legs.
Wing: White polypropylene yarn.
Hackle: Light brown.

WHAT IS IT ABOUT A FLY LIKE THIS THAT CONJURES THE word "fishy?" Maybe it's the sparse trailing shuck, the rubber legs, the full-hackle collar, or the easy-to-spot-on-the-water white wing. Whatever it is, when I first saw this fly, I knew I had to add it to my fly box.

In a couple of key areas, the Grumpy Frumpy reminds me of the famous pattern called the Quigley Cripple: the trailing shuck, forward-facing wing, and hackle collar. However, the addition of the foam back and legs and the change in the body and wing materials seem to make it an entirely new pattern.

Although a little fanciful, the Grumpy Frumpy serves as a fine imitation of an emerging mayfly or a mayfly that fails to successfully emerge. This version has a yellow body, but you can swap colors to tie tan, brown, and olive imitations.

Royal Humpy

Hook: Regular or 2X-long dry-fly hook, sizes 16 to 12.
Thread: Red 8/0.
Tail: Moose hair.
Body: Red thread or floss.
Hump: Elk hair.
Wing: Elk-hair tips.
Hackle: Brown.

THE HUMPY IS A GREAT, CLASSIC DRY FLY YOU'LL FIND IN almost any fly shop. Al and Gretchen Beatty tied this example, so you'll find none better.

The trick to making the Humpy is to first tie the elk hair to the hook before wrapping the thread or floss body; the tips will point toward the rear-end of the fly. Next, wrap the body over the butt ends of the hair. Fold the hair over the top of the body to create the hump, and bend and pinch the tips upright to make the wings. Now you can wrap a full-hackle collar.

The Humpy is a terrific searching pattern for fishing fast currents and pocket water. The red body gives this version the name, Royal Humpy. Switch body colors—use dubbing, floss, peacock herl, etc.—to create your own versions of this timeless pattern.

Poly Humpy

Hook: Regular dry-fly hook, sizes 22 to 6.
Thread: Black 8/0.
Tail: Moose hair.
Body: Red floss.
Hump and wing: Gray polypropylene yarn.
Hackle: Brown.

MAKING A NICE FLY DOESN'T REQUIRE FEATS OF FLY-TYING strength or derring-do; you simply need to place quality materials on the hook in the proper order and proportions to create a durable pattern. If a step is too difficult, sometimes substituting a material simplifies things. A case in point is the Humpy.

The back and wings of the traditional Humpy, which is included in this book, are tied with elk hair. Manipulating the hair over the top of the hook and having the wings come out the correct length, is challenging. Al and Gretchen Beatty's simplified Poly Humpy solves this problem.

Rather than using elk hair, they select polypropylene yarn for the back and wing. The yarn back is easier to fashion, and you simply clip the wings off at the proper length after tying the fly. What could be easier?

Governor

Hook: Regular dry-fly hook, sizes 16 to 12.
Thread: White 8/0.
Tag: Gold tinsel.
Tail: Ginger hackle fibers.
Butt: Red tying thread.
Body: Peacock herl.
Hackle: Ginger.
Wings: Turkey.

I REMEMBER THE DAY I PICKED THROUGH DAVID BRANDT'S
fly boxes, looking for patterns for this project. David is a recognized authority on tying Catskill style dry flies, and he has an encyclopedic knowledge
of the region and the flies. I pointed to this pattern, called the Governor,
and remarked that I was unfamiliar with it.

"That's a very old one," David said, "but it's a dandy. It's also very unusual
in that it's not an imitation, but an attractor pattern."

Indeed, so much has been written about the classic Catskill imitations
of real insects—the Hendrickson, Light Cahill, March Brown, and all the
rest—that most anglers overlook the marvelous attractor flies originated in
that region.

This Governor, with its thick tail and heavy-hackle collar, will float high
and dry over the roughest currents.

EZY Kolzer

Hook: Regular dry-fly hook, sizes 20 to 6.
Thread: Black 8/0.
Tail: Ginger hackle fibers.
Body: Peacock herl or your choice of dubbing.
Body hackle: Brown grizzly.
Wings: Grizzly.
Front hackle: Brown grizzly.

"WHERE DID 'KOLZER' COME FROM IN THE NAME OF THIS pattern?" I asked Al Beatty.

"A guy named John Kolzer tied a dry fly by that name for fishing the McKenzie River. He was from the Pacific Northwest. I learned about it from a book that was published in the early 1950s. We've been tying our version—with the Wonder Wings, and we've lightened the color a bit—for about five years."

Al and Gretchen Beatty do tie perfect flies. The wings and spiral-wrapped hackle are without equal.

Whether used as an imitation or a searching pattern, the EZY Kolzer is one I am adding to my fly box.

Queen of Waters

Hook: Regular dry-fly hook, sizes 14 to 10.
Thread: Tan 8/0.
Tail: Ginger hackle fibers.
Body: Orange floss.
Rib: Gold tinsel.
Hackle: Ginger.
Wing: Mallard-flank fibers.

I AM INCLUDING THE QUEEN OF WATERS, SOMETIMES called the Queen of Water, for two reasons. First, the name of the fly gives our little collection of patterns a touch of class. Second, it highlights the "palmer" style of tying, a technique you can include in many of the flies you tie.

The name, Queen of Waters, hints to the British influence on this fly. Make no mistake, however, that it was once a very popular pattern in the United States, and American authors Theodore Gordon, Rube Cross, and George LaBranche all wrote about it. Note: do not confuse this pattern with a similar pattern, also called Queen of Waters, which is tied as a wet fly.

The palmer style of tying refers to the hackle spiral wrapped up the body. It improves the floatation of a dry fly and increases the buggy appearance of a wet fly. (The Elk-hair Caddis and Stimulator are other dry flies containing palmered hackles.) Catskill angler Rube Cross wrote that the term "palmer" comes from the palmer caterpillar, also known as the palmer worm.

That's a tidbit for conversation at your next fly-fishing cocktail party.

Royal Double Wing

Hook: Standard 2X-long dry-fly hook, sizes 8 to 14.
Thread: Black 6/0 (70 denier).
Tail: Green Antron yarn.
Tip (tag): Red floss.
Body: Peacock herl.
Body Hackle: Brown.
Wing: White calftail.
Butt Wing: Elk hair.
Hackle: Brown.

THIS ATTRACTOR FLY WAS DESIGNED BY FLY-FISHING LEG-
end Gary LaFontaine. Although he said it was an attractor, which means it's
not intended to imitate any specific insect, the Royal Double Wing would
certain be a great choice to match a stonefly.

Curiously, LaFontaine tied this fly in twelve different color combina-
tions to meet every lighting condition: orange for dusk, gray for overcast
days, cream for early morning, yellow for midday, lime for fishing near stre-
ambank vegetation, and more.

Gary recommended the Royal Double Wing for fishing riffles near the
middle of the day. Al and Gretchen Beatty, who supplied this sample of the
pattern, call it "the ultimate attractor."

Since Gary LaFontaine developed the pattern, and the Beattys recommend it so highly, we should add it to our fly boxes.